EXPLORING
THE
MIDDLE
AGES

10

Surgery – Women

Marshall Cavendish
Reference
New York

Marshall Cavendish
99 White Plains Road
Tarrytown, New York 10591-9001

www.marshallcavendish.us

© 2006 Marshall Cavendish Corporation

Contributing authors: Dale Anderson, Jane Bingham, Peter Chrisp, Christopher Gravett, Jen Green, Clare Hibbert, Anne Rooney, Cath Senker, Sean Sheehan, Phil Steele, Paige Weber

MARSHALL CAVENDISH
EDITOR: Thomas McCarthy
EDITORIAL DIRECTOR: Paul Bernabeo
PRODUCTION MANAGER: Michael Esposito

WHITE-THOMSON PUBLISHING
EDITOR: Steven Maddocks
DESIGN: Derek Lee and Ross George
CARTOGRAPHER: Peter Bull Design
PICTURE RESEARCH: Amy Sparks
INDEXER: Cynthia Crippen, AEIOU, Inc.

Library of Congress Cataloging-in-Publication Data
Exploring the Middle Ages.
    p. cm.
    Includes bibliographical references and indexes.
    Contents: 1. Abbasids-battles -- 2. Bayeux tapestry-childbirth and midwifery -- 3. Children-drama -- 4. Education-government -- 5. Greece-India -- 6. Ireland-Mamluks -- 7. Manufacturing-Nan Madol -- 8. Nobility-religion -- 9. Renaissance-sports -- 10. Surgery-women -- 11. Index.
    ISBN 0-7614-7613-X (set: lib. bdg.: alk. paper) -- ISBN 0-7614-7614-8 (v. 1: alk. paper) -- ISBN 0-7614-7615-6 (v. 2: alk. paper) -- ISBN 0-7614-7616-4 (v. 3: alk. paper) -- ISBN 0-7614-7617-2 (v. 4: alk. paper) -- ISBN 0-7614-7618-0 (v. 5: alk. paper) -- ISBN 0-7614-7619-9 (v. 6: alk. paper) -- ISBN 0-7614-7620-2 (v. 7: alk. paper) -- ISBN 0-7614-7621-0 (v. 8: alk. paper) -- ISBN 0-7614-7622-9 (v. 9: alk. paper) -- ISBN 0-7614- 7623-7 (v. 10: alk. paper) -- ISBN 0-7614-7624-5 (v. 11: alk. paper)
    1. Middle Ages--Encyclopedias. 2. Civilization, Medieval--Encyclopedias. I. Marshall Cavendish Corporation.

D114.E88 2006
909.07'03--dc22

                                        2005042161

ISBN 0-7614-7613-X (set)
ISBN 0-7614-7623-7 (vol. 10)

Printed in China

09 08 07 06 05 5 4 3 2 1

color key			
▬▬▬	Africa	▬▬▬	Oceania
▬▬▬	Americas	▬▬▬	South and Southeast Asia
▬▬▬	Central and East Asia	▬▬▬	Western Asia
▬▬▬	Europe	▬▬▬	Cross-cultural articles

Contents

Surgery

SURGERY IS ANY FORM of manual intervention carried out by a medical specialist to heal or change a patient's body. During the Middle Ages surgical practice advanced considerably in the Arab world, where surgeons drew on medical knowledge from India. Nonetheless, in most parts of the world, including Europe, surgery frequently did as much harm as good.

Surgeons in many societies carried out primitive operations, such as the strapping of twisted or broken limbs and amputation.

A baby whose life was in danger might be delivered by Caesarian section (though many mothers failed to survive this procedure). Trepanning, which involved boring or drilling holes in the skull, was thought to relieve pressure on the brain or to allow bad spirits to escape.

Facial Surgery

Indian surgeons developed techniques for rebuilding noses and earlobes around the sixth century BCE. Such reconstructive facial surgery was in high demand, as the cutting off of the nose or ears was a common punishment for crimes in India. These and other surgical techniques are described in the *Susruta-samhita*, a Sanskrit medical work that was translated into Arabic before 900 CE.

Arab Surgeons

Surgery advanced more rapidly in the Arab world than anywhere else. Arab surgeons carried out operations on the main body organs, limbs, blood vessels, and eyes and developed obstetric procedures (obstetrics is the branch of medicine concerned with pregnancy and childbirth). In 997 a hospital founded in Baghdad had twenty-four physicians, a surgery, and a clinic for treating eye disorders.

◀ *A 1345 French illustration whose purpose was to teach students the basics of surgery on the head.*

The Arabs made surgical implements from steel, a noncorroding metal that was easy to clean. They were the first to use cotton to dress and pad wounds and the first to use animal-gut sutures to stitch wounds. They also recognized the need for a detailed study of anatomy as a starting point for developing surgical techniques.

Bloodletting and Barber-Surgeons

Bloodletting, a practice dating from ancient times, was used in the Middle Ages as both cure and therapy. In Europe bloodletting was often carried out by monks, who were familiar with the technique from its regular use as a purification rite in monasteries.

After 1163, when the Council of Tours largely forbade clerics from practicing medicine, bloodletting passed to barbers. Barbers soon took on other simple surgical procedures—tooth extractions, for example—but not till around 1250 (and then only in France) did they get any surgical education.

Around the same time, surgery was first studied in the universities of Europe, where teaching drew extensively on the work of Arab surgeons. The work of London's barber-surgeons was restricted from 1416.

▼ *This anatomical
drawing of the eye
comes from a
thirteenth-century
Arabian manuscript.*

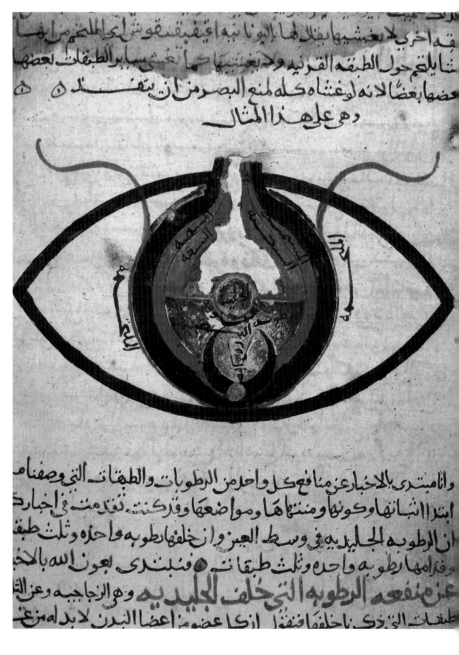

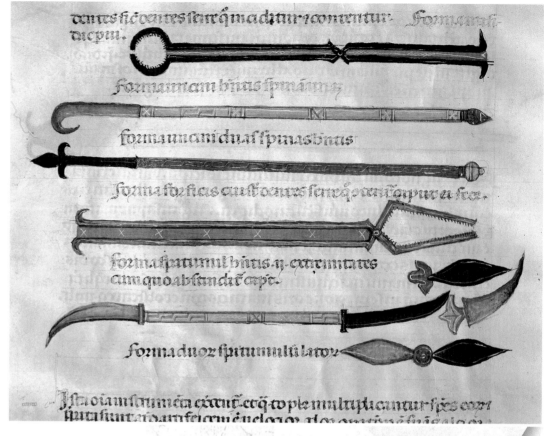

Among the instruments depicted on this page from De chirurgia (On Surgery), a fourteenth-century Latin translation of Albucasis's At-tasrif, are a hook, forceps, and a surgeon's knife.

Pain Relief

In most parts of the world in the Middle Ages, no effective pain relief was available. Delicate procedures were not possible; operations were fast and often brutal.

From the tenth century Arab surgeons anesthetized a patient by holding a sponge soaked in opium or another narcotic over the nose and mouth. Anesthetics, by keeping patients immobile during operations, enabled Arab surgeons to make great advances.

In other areas of the world, wine and other alcoholic drinks were used to dull pain and sedate the patient slightly.

Infection

The causes of infection were not clearly understood during the Middle Ages. Many surgical procedures that might otherwise have succeeded failed because the wound became infected and the patient died.

ALBUCASIS 936–1013

Born near Córdoba, Spain, Abu al-Qasim Khalaf ibn Abbas az-Zahrawi (known in Europe by the Latin form of his name, Albucasis), compiled a large medical encyclopedia, *At-tasrif*, which combines his own work with the fruits of his extensive studies. In the final section, three hundred pages devoted to surgery, he includes the first description and illustrations of two hundred surgical instruments and some illustrations of surgical procedures. *At-tasrif* was used for five hundred years in the Middle East and Europe. Among the procedures that Albucasis describes are how to reimplant teeth, fit false teeth made of cow bone, strip varicose veins, remove kidney stones, and perform a tracheotomy.

Methods for cleaning wounds included washing with wine or vinegar, using maggots to eat away rotten flesh, and cauterizing (sealing with a hot metal rod). A less traumatic alternative to cauterization involved tying off the ends of blood vessels with fine thread, a method developed by Albucasis.

SEE ALSO
• Childbirth and Midwifery
• Disease
• Ibn Sina
• Medicine and Healing
• Science

Sweden

THE PRESENT-DAY COUNTRY OF SWEDEN occupies most of the Scandinavian Peninsula. During the ninth century Swedish Vikings established colonies in eastern Europe and Russia. A united kingdom by the early eleventh century, Sweden expanded eastward and absorbed parts of Finland and Russia. In 1397 the Kalmar Union created a single Scandinavian state, but the union disintegrated in 1523.

Pagan Times

Sweden is named for the Swedes, or Svea, a people who settled around Lake Mälaren, in eastern Sweden, in the sixth century. By the seventh century the Swedes had gained power over the Götar and other neighboring tribes.

The Viking Age began around 800. Many Swedes began both migrating and raiding in search of goods—principally furs, slaves, and dirhems (Arab silver coins)— and new trade routes. They settled lands to the south, east, and west and traveled as far afield as Baghdad. Swedish Vikings founded a trading post at Kiev, in present-day Ukraine, around 860.

Christianity and Kings

In the early ninth century the missionary Saint Ansgar (c. 801–865) established a church at Birka. However, worship of the old Viking gods did not die out until the reign of Erik Jedvarsson (d. 1160), around the time that Sweden's first archbishop was appointed. Uppsala Cathedral, begun in 1285, took 150 years to complete. One of Sweden's most famous saints was the mystic Bridget (c. 1303–1373), who founded an order of nuns in 1370.

Conflicting Forces

In 1318 the Swedish nobles drove King Birger into exile. The following year they invited the Norwegian king, Magnus VII, to rule them as Magnus II of Sweden (he reigned until 1355 in Norway and until 1363 in Sweden). In 1397 the Kalmar Union officially joined together Denmark, Norway, and Sweden.

During the fifteenth century some Swedes grew unhappy with Danish rule. Denmark in turn became unhappy about Swedish links with the Hanseatic League, an alliance of German traders. In 1520, after Danish forces beheaded eighty Swedish nobles and burghers, the Swedes

▲ *This shield boss dates from between 550 and 800, a period of Swedish history known as the Vendel Period, after a cemetery near Vendel, Uppland. Many Svea chieftains were buried at Vendel inside boats packed with belongings for use in the afterlife.*

In 1370 Saint Bridget of Sweden founded an order of nuns called the Brigittines; its chief convent was at Vadstena. Bridget (right) is depicted on this twelfth-century Danish altarpiece with Saint Thecla.

rebelled. The leader of the rebellion, Gustav Vasa, founded a dynasty that ruled Sweden for the next 130 years.

Way of Life

Most Swedes lived in farming and fishing villages. They raised animals, grew grain, and caught sprats and herring. Swedish artisans worked with leather, wood, bronze, iron, and textiles. Birka and Sigtuna, both on Lake Mälaren, were the earliest trading centers. From the thirteenth century the key ports were Stockholm, positioned where Lake Mälaren meets the Baltic Sea, and Visby, a town on the island of Götland that was controlled by the Hanseatic League.

A VIKING TOWN

Birka was founded around 760 on an island in the center of Lake Mälaren. For two hundred years it was an important trading center where silver and pearls from the east were traded for Scandinavian iron and skins. At its peak Birka's population numbered around seven hundred. By the tenth century the channels linking Lake Mälaren to the Baltic Sea had become too shallow for seagoing vessels, and so traders moved to the growing coastal town of Stockholm.

SEE ALSO

- Denmark
- Hanseatic League
- Norway
- Novgorod
- Sagas
- Vikings

CHRONOLOGY

c. 600
The Svea settle around Lake Mälaren.

1164
Sweden's first archbishopric is established at Uppsala.

1319
Sweden unites with Norway.

1350
The Black Death kills approximately one-third of Sweden's population.

1397
The Kalmar Union unites Denmark, Norway, and Sweden.

1520
Swedes overthrow the Danes; Gustav Vasa, the leader of the rebellion, founds a Swedish ruling dynasty.

1523
The Kalmar Union is dissolved.

Swiss Confederation

THE PEOPLE OF MEDIEVAL SWITZERLAND did not belong to a single state; they lived in cantons, separate self-governing communities. Joining together for mutual protection in the late thirteenth century, the cantons began to form a loose grouping called the Confederation. After winning independence from the Holy Roman Empire, the Swiss Confederation became one of the strongest military powers in Europe.

From the eleventh century Switzerland was part of the Holy Roman Empire, a territory ruled by German kings that stretched from the North Sea to northern Italy. The emperors, generally weak rulers, allowed the Swiss cantons to govern themselves. In 1273, however, Rudolf of Hapsburg was elected emperor. The Hapsburgs were powerful local lords; they intended to exercise direct control of their Swiss subjects. In the 1270s Schwyz, Unterwalden, and Uri, three cantons in the forest region of Waldstätte, formed a secret pact of mutual defense.

Following the death of Rudolf in July 1291, the forest cantons renewed their pact in a public ceremony. In August 1291 they met on the Rütli meadow, by Lake Lucerne, where they swore for all time to "aid and defend each other . . . against every enemy whatever who shall attempt to molest them, either singly or collectively." This oath marks the formal beginning of the Swiss Confederation.

Following the oath, conflict between the Swiss and agents of the Hapsburgs intensified. One positive consequence of

◀ *This woodcut— from a version of the story of William Tell published around 1500—shows the founding event of the Swiss Confederation, the famous oath taken in 1291 by representatives of the forest cantons on the Rütli meadow.*

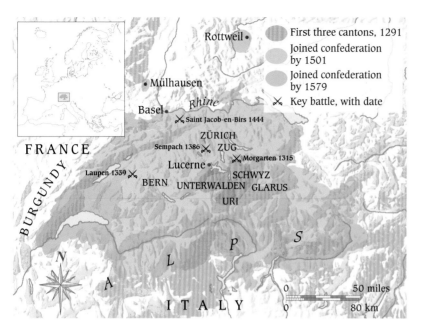

Rottweil •

First three cantons, 1291
Joined confederation by 1501
Joined confederation by 1579
Key battle, with date

Mülhausen •

Basel •   *Rhine*

✕ Saint Jacob-en-Birs 1444

ZÜRICH

Sempach 1386 ✕   ZUG

Lucerne •   ✕ Morgarten 1315

Laupen 1339 ✕

BERN   SCHWYZ

UNTERWALDEN   GLARUS

URI

FRANCE

BURGUNDY

A   L   P   S

N

ITALY

0   50 miles
0   80 km

▲ *A landlocked country with no natural defensive boundaries, medieval Switzerland was threatened by powerful neighbors. The Swiss response to this threat was to form a confederation of cantons.*

this conflict for the Swiss was the birth of a legend of a freedom fighter named William Tell, first written down in the fifteenth century. In the legend, as punishment for disobeying a wicked Hapsburg official, Tell is forced to shoot an apple from his son's head with a bow and arrow.

The Battle of Morgarten

In November 1315, Leopold, the Hapsburg duke of Austria, led an invading army of two thousand knights and seven thousand foot soldiers into the valley of Schwyz. At Morgarten, where the road passed between a lake and a steep wooded slope, the Swiss had prepared a trap by blocking the road with logs. Hidden in the forest above, 1,300 Swiss fighters lay in wait. As soon as the first knights reached the wall of logs and were forced to halt, the Swiss charged down the slope. Unaware of what lay ahead, the

Austrians in the rear continued to advance. The knights in front, by now so hemmed in that they could barely use their weapons, were slaughtered by the Swiss.

Growth

The cantons took advantage of their victory at Morgarten to strengthen and expand the Confederation. In 1332 the town of Lucerne rebelled against its Hapsburg overlords and joined the Confederation. In 1339 the Confederation made a military alliance with Bern, which was under threat from the Burgundians. At the Battle of Laupen in 1339, a combined army from Bern and the Confederation decisively defeated a much larger army from Burgundy. Bern formally joined the Confederation in the 1350s, along with Zürich, Zug, and Glarus. In 1386 the Swiss won another great victory over the Hapsburgs at the Battle of Sempach, where 1,600 Swiss troops defeated 6,000 Austrians.

The Mad Battle

As well as being tough and disciplined, the Swiss had a reputation for complete fearlessness that would make them the most valued mercenary soldiers in Europe. In 1444 the French invaded Switzerland with an army of 30,000 men. At Saint-Jacob-en-Birs, they were met by a force of just 1,200 Swiss pikemen. Undismayed by the size of the enemy force, the Swiss attacked. They charged headlong into the French army and

CHRONOLOGY

1291
Uri, Schwyz, and Unterwalden publicly renew their pact.

1315
The Battle of Morgarten is fought.

1332
Lucerne joins the Swiss Confederation.

1351–1353
Zürich, Glarus, Zug, and Bern join the confederation.

1386
The Swiss defeat the Austrians at the Battle of Sempach.

1444
The Battle of Saint-Jacob-en-Birs is fought.

1474–1477
Swiss fight Burgundians and win control of Alsace.

1499
The Treaty of Basel guarantees Swiss independence.

SWISS FIGHTING METHODS

The Swiss fought on foot with pikes (spears with an extremely long shaft) and halberds. A halberd was a six-foot (1.8 m) shaft mounted with a spear point with a hatchet and spike on either side of it; the halberd could be jabbed like a pike, swung like a battle-ax, and used to hook a rider from his horse. The Swiss advanced in a tight mass, shoulder to shoulder, and marched in step to the beat of a drum. The success of Swiss tactics was demonstrated at the Battle of Laupen (1339), where foot soldiers drove a larger Burgundian cavalry force from the battlefield—an extremely infrequent occurrence.

fought bravely until the last Swiss soldier had been killed. Yet the Swiss inflicted so many casualties that the French abandoned their planned invasion.

A European Power

During the fifteen century the Swiss Confederation developed into a great European power that was able to expand abroad. Individual cantons increased their territory through conquest. Uri expanded south as far as Italy, while Bern expanded north to the Rhine River. From 1474 to 1477, the Confederation fought a victorious war against Burgundy and won Alsace. In the 1490s the Swiss fought yet another war against a Hapsburg ruler, Emperor Maximilian I. This war ended with the 1499 Treaty of Basel, in which Maximilian agreed to recognize Swiss independence.

◄ *This chronicle illustration of around 1450 shows Swiss foot soldiers with pikes falling on the Austrian knights at the Battle of Morgarten. The picture mistakenly shows the Swiss wearing full body armor. In fact, it was their lack of armor that allowed the Swiss to move so quickly.*

SEE ALSO
- **Hapsburgs**
- **Holy Roman Empire**
- **Warfare**

Synagogues

A SYNAGOGUE IS A PLACE where Jews gather, primarily to worship but also to study religious texts and engage in discussion. The word derives from the Greek *synagein*, meaning "to bring people together." In the Middle Ages synagogues were built wherever there was a Jewish community sizable and secure enough to support its existence.

▼ This image from a Jewish religious text, the Barcelona Hagadda, dates from around 1350 and depicts a rabbi reading from the Torah in a synagogue; the Hebrew script is from Psalm 113.

The precise origin of synagogues is uncertain, but it is possible that they date from the period of exile in Babylon, after the Jews were expelled from Jerusalem in 586 BCE. The synagogue assumed its vital role in the preservation and development of Judaism after the fall of the Second Temple—and with it the established Jewish priesthood—in Jerusalem in 70 CE.

Medieval Synagogues

The medieval synagogue was generally small and modest. A twelfth-century synagogue in Guildford, in southern England, for example, was only about ten feet (3 m) square. A synagogue usually had seats on three sides, with separate seating areas for men and women. The fourth side faced Jerusalem. The most important feature, the ark that contained the Torah scrolls, was placed at the front. Above the ark was the *ner tamid,* the perpetual light, and in the center was the bimah, the raised platform from which prayers and passages from the Torah were read.

Prayers were generally sung unaccompanied by musical instruments. The Jews of the Byzantine Empire were influenced by the dominant Greek culture; in Byzantine synagogues the Torah was read in Greek translation rather than in the traditional Hebrew.

Synagogues under Attack

As the focus of the Jewish community, a synagogue was prone to attack wherever Jews were subject to persecution. From the end of the fourth century, owing to pressure from the growing Christian church, Roman imperial laws were enacted to prevent the erection of new synagogues. (There were other laws, however, that protected the right of Jews to maintain their places of worship.) Nevertheless, the period from the

THE SYNAGOGUE OF CÓRDOBA

A synagogue was constructed in Córdoba in 1315, when the city was under Christian rule. It remained in use until the expulsion of the Jews from Spain in 1492. This period saw a great intermingling of Jewish, Christian, and Muslim culture in Spain. This cultural mix was represented in the synagogue. The interior was beautifully decorated by Mudejar artists, Spanish Muslims under Christian rule. There were several star ornaments in the Arab style, and the walls were covered with inscriptions from the Psalms (the book of sacred songs in the Hebrew scriptures).

fourth through the seventh century was a golden age for synagogue construction.

Synagogues in the Islamic World

In the Islamic Empire, Jews were for the most part tolerated and permitted to build synagogues. The Ben-Ezra Synagogue, for instance, was built in Al-Fustat (Old Cairo) in 882. Pilgrims from around North Africa visited the synagogue, and large-scale celebrations were held there after the Passover and Sukkoth festivals. However, at times Jews living in Islamic territories suffered persecution. In the early eleventh century, a wave of anti-Jewish and anti-Christian riots swept through Palestine and Egypt. Churches and synagogues were desecrated, and in 1012 the Al-Fustat synagogue was destroyed.

Conflict and Destruction

Jews in Europe were often at odds with those among whom they lived. Violence

▲ *This picture of a Catholic church (left) and a Jewish synagogue comes from a 1023 manuscript of* De Universo, *an encyclopedia written by the German theologian Rabanus Maurus between 842 and 847.*

against them was not uncommon, and synagogues were frequent targets. Guildford's synagogue was razed around 1270. Similar destruction took place in Austria in 1420, when Jews were expelled from Vienna and their property was confiscated.

SEE ALSO
- Byzantine Empire • Córdoba, Emirate of
- Festivals, Religious • Judaism • Religion
- Spanish Kingdoms

Tang Dynasty

THE PERIOD OF THE TANG DYNASTY (618–907 CE) is considered a golden age in Chinese history. Under the Tang the Chinese Empire stretched from central Asia in the west to Korea in the east. Traders, ambassadors, artists, and scholars from all over Asia traveled to the Tang capital, Chang'an, one of the known world's most cosmopolitan cities. The Tang developed a meritocratic civil service and created a great law code that formed the basis of many later East Asian legal systems.

Fall of the Sui

The Tang built on the achievements of the short-lived Sui dynasty (581–617), whose rulers reunited China after centuries of disunity. Sui rule broke down in the early seventh century after a disastrous attempt to conquer Koguryu, in northern Korea. From 613 there were widespread rebellions that the central government was unable to suppress. In 617 the leading Sui general, Li Yüan, rose in revolt, determined to restore order. The following year, when the last Sui emperor was murdered by his own officials, Li Yüan proclaimed a new dynasty, the Tang. Now known as Gaozu ("high forefather"), the name given to him after death, the first Tang emperor spent most of his reign defeating his rivals and restoring peace and order throughout China.

Gaozu nationalized and redistributed Chinese land. He granted every able-bodied male peasant an equal-sized plot.

By around 750 the Tang had established in China a stable and prosperous empire whose cultural and political influence spread far beyond its borders. In central Asia, where the Tang had numerous military protectorates, Arab Muslim influence began to assert itself from the late 700s. Further threats to Chinese stability came from the steppe peoples to the north.

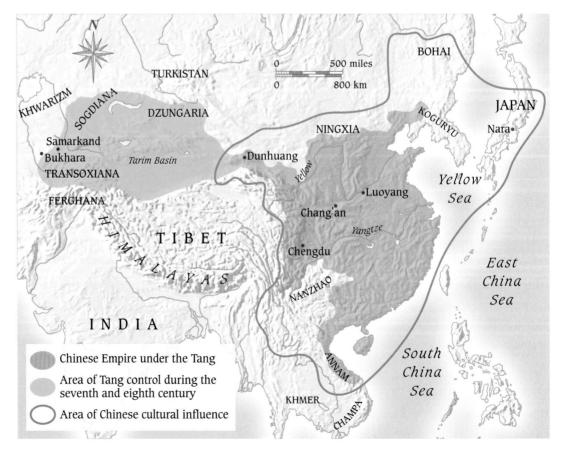

Chinese Empire under the Tang

Area of Tang control during the seventh and eighth century

Area of Chinese cultural influence

In return, peasants were required to pay part of their crop in tax and were liable to be conscripted into the army or made to work on building schemes.

For a model of how to govern China, the Tang looked back to the Han dynasty (206 BCE–220 CE). They revived the Han system of administering the country with a professional civil service, in which promotion depended on the passing of examinations. The aristocracy, which had controlled public appointments since the fall of the Han, declined in power.

Taizong

The second Tang emperor, Taizong (reigned 626–649), succeeded to the throne after murdering two brothers and forcing his father to abdicate. In the process of expanding the empire into central Asia, Taizong defeated the western Turks and conquered the Tarim Basin. In 639 he boasted, "I with my three-foot sword, have pacified all within the four seas, and the barbarians from distant places have come to submit, one after the other."

Empress Wu

Taizong was succeeded by his son, Gaozong (reigned 649–683), a weak and sickly man who was dominated by his empress, Wu Zetian. After 660, when Gaozong suffered a stroke, Wu made herself effective ruler of China. On Gaozong's death in 683, she ruled through two of her sons before proclaiming herself empress in 690. The reign of Wu, the only female sovereign in Chinese history, ended in 705. Under her rule, the empire reached its greatest extent.

▶ *On this silk painting the second Tang emperor, Taizong, is pictured studying a medical text.*

A keen promoter of Buddhism, Empress Wu built monasteries and encouraged monks to translate Buddhist texts. In return, Buddhist monks gave her political support and claimed that she was an incarnation of Maitreya, the future Buddha. Buddhist monasteries became government-run institutions as well as powerful and wealthy landowners.

High Tang Poetry

The arts, especially literature, flourished in Tang China. More than 48,000 poems survive from the period of Tang rule. The finest were written during the eighth century, a period known as the High, or Flourishing, Tang. Du Fu (712–770) is generally considered to be the greatest of all Chinese poets. Du Fu wrote more than two hundred reflective poems. In many of them, he gives eloquent voice to his concern for the sufferings of the poor.

The An Lushan Rebellion

In 755 An Lushan, the military governor of northeastern China, fearing that the chief minister was about to dismiss him, rebelled against the government. He quickly captured the eastern capital and the following year declared himself emperor of a new dynasty, called the Great Yen. Although An Lushan was assassinated in 757, the rebellion he started was continued by his sons and officers for a further six years.

The An Lushan rebellion left large areas of the most productive lands in China devastated and depopulated. With frontier

▶ *Tang imperial tombs often contain small pottery guardian figures trampling demons. Based on guardian statues from Sri Lankan Buddhist temples, these figures were supposed to protect the tomb from evil spirits.*

THE TANG DYNASTY

618–626	Gaozu		**762–780**	Daizong
626–649	Taizong		**780–805**	Dezong
649–683	Gaozong		**805–806**	Shunzong
683	Zhongzong (forced to abdicate after one month, in favor of his brother, by his mother, Wu)		**806–821**	Xianzong
			821–825	Muzong
683–690	Ruizong (placed on the throne by his mother, Wu, and then deposed by her)		**825–826**	Jingzong
			826–840	Wenzong
690–705	Wu Zetian		**840–846**	Wuzong
705–710	Zhongzong (restored to the throne by Wu's ministers and generals and later forced to resign)		**846–859**	Xuanzong
			859–874	Yizong
710–712	Ruizong (restored by a coup led by his son, Xuanzong)		**874–889**	Xizong
			889–904	Zhaozong
712–756	Xuanzong (forced off the throne by An Lushan)		**904–907**	Aidi (Zhaoxuan)
756–762	Suzong			

armies withdrawn to defend the center, the Tibetans were able to overrun the northeast.

Buddhism Suppressed

In 845 Emperor Wuzong (reigned 840–846) issued an edict suppressing Buddhism and other foreign religions. He declared that "the temples of the empire that have been demolished number more than 4,600; 26,500 monks and nuns have been returned to lay life . . . more than 100,000 idle and unproductive Buddhist followers have been expelled, and countless of their gaudy useless buildings destroyed."

Wuzong was influenced by Taoist priests, who held out to him the promise of the secret of immortality and urged him to suppress their rivals. An equally important factor in the emperor's decision was his desire to seize the vast estates held by the Buddhist monasteries. Although Buddhism survived as a popular Chinese religion, it never regained the power it had held under the early Tang rulers.

During the Tang period the Chinese learned to make porcelain using powdered stone and kaolin (white china clay). This white translucent porcelain bowl was found in a Tang-era tomb.

Fall of the Dynasty

The late ninth century saw widespread peasant uprisings. At the same time, provincial generals were becoming increasingly independent. By 907, when the last Tang emperor fell from power, China had broken up into ten separate states.

SEE ALSO
- Chang'an • China • Crime and Punishment
- Silk Road

Taxes and Tithes

IN ITS COMMONEST FORM a tax is a sum of money imposed on the public by a ruler or government in order to finance activities of state. Taxes may also be paid in the form of goods, services, or labor. As a successful state depends on tax revenue, its governors must be able to enforce and implement an efficient system of taxation. A tithe (literally, "tenth part") was a tax levied by the medieval church for its support.

The power of the Roman Empire was founded as much on tax collection as on the force of arms. After the collapse of the western empire in 476 CE, Europe's warrior bands funded their activities through pillage and extortion. To stabilize their territory, new kingdoms and empires needed to reinstitute formal systems of taxation. In many places this process took several cen-

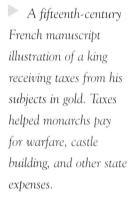 A fifteenth-century French manuscript illustration of a king receiving taxes from his subjects in gold. Taxes helped monarchs pay for warfare, castle building, and other state expenses.

turies, and extortionate taxes led repeatedly to civil unrest in the late Middle Ages.

Types of Taxation

A direct tax may be levied on an individual or an institution. An indirect tax may be levied on transactions, sales, services, or land. Both forms of taxation were commonly imposed by monarchs and other authorities.

In the Byzantine Empire taxes were levied on land and produce, on inheritance, on the purchase of goods, and on imports and exports. Some taxes were designed as methods of social engineering. In the Turkish Ottoman Empire, for example, unmarried men had to pay an extra tax until their wedding day.

In the feudal system of western Europe, a strict social hierarchy was cemented not only by oaths of duty and service but also by financial payments. In England a lowly peasant, or villein, sometimes had to pay his feudal lord an annual tax, a tallage, as well as occasional taxes called reliefs—levied, for example, upon the taking over of a new landholding. He would also have to pay a tax on grain ground into flour at the lord's mill. A person who owed the king military service could pay scutage (shield tax) instead of providing knights. A monarch might levy a specific tax to pay for a war or to pay the ransom of those captured by the enemy.

Methods of Payment

In the Middle Ages monetary tax was generally in the form of coins, which were stored in heavy chests and transported by wagon. In China paper money was introduced in the year 812 as a means of forwarding tax revenue from the provinces to the capital more easily.

In many countries local taxes were often paid in kind—that is, in the form of livestock, crops, or produce. A tax might be paid in a form of public service known as corvée. In China and the Incan Empire of

TAX REBELLIONS

Excessive taxation caused violent rebellions in fourteenth-century Europe. In the 1370s England was waging a costly war with France, and the king sought to raise revenue through taxation. At that time common taxes included customs charges on the wool, cloth, and wine trades and taxes on movable property, known as tenths, fifteenths, and so on, according to the proportion of a person's revenue that was paid. A poll (head) tax was levied on individuals for the first time in England in 1377 and again in 1379 and 1380. In 1381 large numbers of English people refused to pay. The resulting investigation provoked the violent Peasants' Revolt.

▲ *This woodcut of 1479 depicts people paying a tithe to the church. Tithes were enforced under a statute of the Frankish emperor Charlemagne (742–814) and continued to be levied throughout the Middle Ages.*

**CO̅TADOR·MAIOR·I·TE3ORERO
TAVANTIN·SVIO·QVIPOC
CVRACA·CON DOR·CHAVA**

◁ *An Incan tax official uses a quipu. The colored cords could represent anything from households to stores of grain. Knots represented numbers.*

Peru, peasants had to devote periods of their life to building roads, bridges, or walls for the state. In Peru the weaving of textiles also counted as *mit'a*, or labor tax.

Administering Taxation

Before imposing taxation, a government often needed to gather information about the size and location of the population and about landholdings and transactions. In England, by 1086 King William I had compiled the Domesday Book, a register of population, land, and livestock for most of the country. The book was used for tax assessment until 1522. In medieval China a vast civil service administered censuses, registered land, and collected taxes.

Religious Taxes

In many parts of the world, taxes were levied not just by kings and feudal lords but also by religious bodies. Jewish and Christian scriptures urged the faithful to set aside a tenth part—a tithe—of their produce for God's use; in medieval Europe the tithe became a formal tax imposed by the church. Crops given to the church were stored in village tithe barns. In the Incan Empire one-third of every harvest was given to the priestly class. In early medieval China, Buddhist monasteries and temples were exempted from state taxes and funded by public donations.

SEE ALSO

TALLY STICKS AND QUIPUS

In medieval England the king's accounts were settled publicly on a checkered cloth known as the *scaccarium,* or exchequer. State finances became known collectively as the Exchequer, a term still used in Britain. Tax records were kept on parchment scrolls. Receipts were issued in the form of tallies, sticks on which carved notches represented sums of money. The sticks were split; one half was retained by the tax collector, and the other by the person being taxed. The two sections could later be compared to see if they matched, or tallied. In Incan Peru records of population, corvée labor, and taxes in kind were recorded on a quipu, an ingenious system of knotted and colored cords.

Temples

A TEMPLE IS A RELIGIOUS MONUMENT or building dedicated to one or more deities or other sacred figures. Temples may be used for rituals, ceremonies, offerings, dances, or festivals and often contain religious statues or shrines. In contrast with synagogues, churches, and mosques, temples are not necessarily used for communal worship.

The ancient temples of Europe, North Africa, and western Asia were no longer used as such in the medieval period, although some were taken over by newer faiths. For example, the Pantheon, a temple built in Rome in 124 CE, was converted to a Christian church in 609.

The Americas

Temples in the Americas took the form of flat-topped pyramids, platforms, or mounds. In North America rectangular flat-topped mounds, some over one hundred feet (30 m) high with wooden buildings on top, were raised by town dwellers in the Mississippi valley. The culture of the worshipers—peoples known collectively as the Southern Cult—developed from about 700 and peaked around 1250.

In Mexico and Central America stepped pyramids towered above large cities. The Temple of the Sun at Teotihuacán, a city whose population numbered around 200,000 in 500 CE, was a center of pilgrimage.

The city of Tikal, rebuilt by the Maya around 700, had five temple pyramids.

Platform-mound temples were built on the South American coast from about 2600 BCE. This tradition continued at Chan Chan, Peru, the great city of the Chimú empire, which thrived from the eighth to the fifteenth century CE, and at Tiwanaku, Bolivia, which was at the height of its power from about 600 to 1000.

Other architectural features in South America included a ceremonial arch (the Gateway of the Sun at Tiwanaku, for instance) and a compound containing gabled stone buildings whose interiors were adorned with golden images (the Incan Temple of the Sun at Cuzco, Peru, for instance).

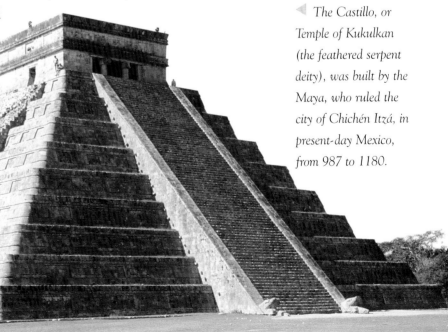

◀ *The Castillo, or Temple of Kukulkan (the feathered serpent deity), was built by the Maya, who ruled the city of Chichén Itzá, in present-day Mexico, from 987 to 1180.*

This statue of Vishnu dominates a Hindu shrine at Badami, in southwestern India. Cave temples were carved here from sandstone under the sixth-century Chalukya dynasty.

Indian Temples and Towers

Hindu temples in India were built in a number of architectural styles. The basic design featured a sanctuary with a portico embellished with ornate sculpture. The temple at Deoghar, in northeastern India, which was dedicated to the god Shiva in about 600, is an example of this design. Around the same time, caves were being converted into temples, the pillars and elaborately carved figures hewn directly from the rock. Indeed cave temples, common to Hindus and Buddhists, were used as early as the first century CE. Examples survive at Badami, in southwestern India, and Ajanta and Ellora, in south-central India.

During the reign of the Pallava dynasty, there were a number of innovations in southern Indian temple building. Notable additions were a large hall for sacred dance and a tall pyramid-shaped tower, the *shikhara*, which rose in tiers. The eighth-century Shore Temple at Mamallapuram is typical. A great age of southern Indian temple building began under the Cholas in the eleventh and twelfth centuries. Between about 1100 and 1350, high gate towers (*gopurams*) were added to many Hindu temples.

Temple Complexes of Southeast Asia

In Burma (present-day Myanmar) the conversion of King Anawratha to Buddhism in 1056 heralded a period of intensive temple building. In an area of just 16.2 square miles (42 km²) around Anawratha's capital, Bagan, the remains of 2,217 temples survive. Angkor Wat, in Cambodia, is the largest religious structure ever constructed, its outer walls enclosing an area of 403 acres (163 hectares). Built between 1115 and 1150, Angkor Wat was dedicated to the Hindu god Vishnu by the Khmer king Suryavarman II.

China and Japan

In medieval China, Confucian, Taoist, and Buddhist traditions greatly influenced one another. Since geomancy (a form of divination by means of geographical features) and numerology dominated the Taoist tradition, factors such as location, orientation, building materials, design, and the number of steps all assumed great spiritual significance. Temple sites often included a series of courtyards, bridges, and steps. Painted and tiled wooden halls, with pillars and decorative eaves, contained shrines and statues. A typical example is the Buddhist Foguang Si, in Shaanxi Province (built in 857).

In Japan, where the native religion was Shintoism, simple early shrines had developed by the Middle Ages into more complex temple compounds entered through a torii, a sacred gateway. Shinto architecture was later influenced by Chinese Buddhist designs, which were first

FROM STUPA TO PAGODA

The Aryan peoples who colonized northern India in ancient times buried their leaders under large mounds topped by a badge of rank that resembled a multitiered umbrella. Indian Buddhists adopted the mound shape in the form of a stupa, a stone dome enclosing sacred relics, around which processions were staged. The emblem at the top evolved into the temple tower, or *shikhara*, which was a feature of Hindu temples. A similar design adopted in China was commonly used in Buddhist temples after 523 CE in the form of a pagoda, a slender multistoried tower with a series of projecting eaves.

▲ *The Golden Pavilion was built in Kyoto, Japan, by the shogun Yoshimitsu. It became a temple after his death in 1408.*

adopted in Japan in the Asuka period (538–645). These later designs included both pagodas and halls.

Japanese Buddhist temples became increasingly elaborate, until the austere Zen sect took hold in the Kamakura period (1185–1337), at which time statues were removed, natural wood replaced paintwork, and roofs were built lower.

SEE ALSO

- Aztecs
- Buddhism
- Cholas
- Hinduism
- Incas
- India
- Religion

Thomas Aquinas

THE ITALIAN THEOLOGIAN, scholar, and teacher Thomas Aquinas (1225–1274) brought the teachings of the ancient Greek philosopher Aristotle into Christian doctrine. His most important work, the monumental *Summa theologica* (begun in 1266), has been described as a cathedral of theology on account of its vast scope and lofty design. Aquinas's work was so influential that for centuries after his death, Thomism, the system of thought he created, remained one of the main branches of philosophy.

▶ *In this painted panel by Giovanni Battista the Elder, Thomas Aquinas wears the habit of a Dominican monk. He is often described as being a tall and rather large man. When he was young, his studious silence, combined with his size, led his fellow students to think him dim-witted and nickname him the Dumb Ox.*

The name Aquinas ("of Aquino") denotes Thomas's southern Italian birthplace. At age five he was placed in the Benedictine monastery of Monte Cassino as an oblate (a form of thanksgiving or repentance on the part of his parents). He returned to his parents in 1239, when the Holy Roman emperor expelled the monks for being too loyal to the pope.

While studying at the University of Naples, Aquinas first encountered Greek philosophical works. In 1244 he entered the Dominican order, which had been founded thirty years earlier. The Dominicans believed that a monk should follow an active and useful career. They sent Aquinas to Paris, where he was taught by the German scholar now usually called Albertus Magnus (Albert the Great; c. 1200–1280). As well as teaching at the University of Paris, Albert established a Dominican center of learning at Cologne.

In 1256 Aquinas received his license to teach. He spent the rest of his life teaching in Paris (1256–1259 and 1269–1272) and Italy (1259–1269 and 1272–1274). During his career Aquinas created a curriculum for Dominican studies. He died in March 1274 while traveling to the Council of Lyons, where he was to serve as an adviser to Pope Gregory X. Pope John XXII canonized Aquinas in 1323.

THOMIST PROOFS OF GOD'S EXISTENCE

Aquinas stated that "reason does not destroy faith but perfects it." In one reasoned proof of the existence of God, Aquinas argues that any moving object—from a falling apple to a planet—must have been set in motion by another object or force. He reasons that the very first moving object was set in motion by a Prime Mover, or Unmoved Mover—God.

Using a similar argument, Aquinas reasons that nothing can create itself. Instead, everything must have been created or caused by another, previously existing thing. This chain of causation or existence goes back as far as the first Uncaused Cause—again, God.

Works and Influence

Aquinas was the foremost thinker of his time at the University of Paris. The *Summa theologica,* written in Latin and running to over a million words, covers a huge range of issues regarding Christian belief and practice with an amazing sureness of touch and attention to detail.

Aquinas defended the Christian faith using the principles of logic and reason set out in the writings of the ancient Greek philosopher Aristotle (384–322 BCE). Aquinas argued that faith and reason could be compatible—a radical view shared by the Jewish philosopher Maimonides. In the *Summa theologica,* which he never completed, Aquinas intended to rationalize the Virgin Birth, the Resurrection, and all the other Christian mysteries.

One of Aquinas's central arguments for the existence of God was the necessity of a Prime Mover, a Creator who had set the world in motion. This view was rejected by the Scottish Franciscan philosopher John Duns Scotus (c. 1266–1308), another of the so-called Scholastics, or Schoolmen, who taught at Paris. Aquinas and Scotus both had large followings, and until the sixteenth century their successors, called Thomists and Scotists, wielded great influence. Thomism enjoyed a revival toward

▲ Aquinas's earliest studies were at the Abbey of Monte Cassino, near Aquino. His parents hoped he would one day become abbot there, but Aquinas chose instead to become a Dominican friar.

the end of the nineteenth century, when the Catholic Church expressed renewed interest in Aquinas's writings. His theology was given pride of place in Catholic thinking, a position it still officially holds.

SEE ALSO

- Maimonides • Mendicants • Paris
- Philosophy • Religion
- Roman Catholic Church • Universities

Thousand and One Nights

ALSO KNOWN AS THE *ARABIAN NIGHTS*, the *Thousand and One Nights* is one of the most important works of medieval literature. A collection of stories with no single identifiable author, the *Thousand and One Nights* includes some widely known fictional characters, such as Sindbad the Sailor, as well as the Abbasid caliph Harun ar-Rashid (reigned 786–809) and other historical figures.

Structure and Content

The *Thousand and One Nights* has a frame story that holds together all the separate tales. The frame story concerns King Shahryar, who believes all women are untrustworthy and so has vowed never to let any of his wives survive beyond their wedding night. For three years he kills each new wife, until he marries Scheherazade. Scheherazade comes up with the ploy of telling him fascinating stories, many of which involve magical encounters—especially with spirits called *jinn* (the Arabic word from which *genie* is derived). In certain places a character within a story starts telling a tale of his or her own.

The Changing Tales

The sources of the *Thousand and One Nights* include folktales from India, Persia, Greece, Egypt, and China, which were originally passed on orally. The various tales were first brought together as the Persian *Hazar afsana* (*One Thousand Legends*) and translated into Arabic during the eighth

◀ *This fourteenth-century illumination depicts Sindbad the Sailor on the fifth of his seven voyages. On his shoulders he carries the shape-shifting Old Man of the Sea.*

century as *Alf laylah (One Thousand Nights)*. During the ninth century an expanded version of *Alf laylah* appeared, and in the tenth century popular Egyptian tales were added. By the sixteenth century the collection also included stories brought from China to the Middle East by the Mongols.

Legacy

The *Thousand and One Nights* is the best-known medieval Arabic work of fiction. Versions survive in beautiful manuscripts illustrated by some of the period's finest illuminators. The work was not introduced to the West until the early eighteenth century, when it was translated by the Frenchman Antoine Galland. Galland introduced some new stories,

▲ *Genies (in Arabic,* jinn) *feature prominently in the* Thousand and One Nights. *Here, they carry their princess, Badi' al-Jamal, up into the air with her beloved, the Egyptian prince Saif ul-Muluk.*

including those of Ali Baba and Aladdin. The most famous and widely read translation into English was made by the explorer and scholar Richard Francis Burton in the late 1880s.

The *Thousand and One Nights* remains popular and highly influential around the world. It has inspired poems, paintings, operas, orchestral pieces, pantomimes, ballets, and numerous movies.

SCHEHERAZADE'S GIFT FOR STORYTELLING SAVES HER FROM EXECUTION BY HER HUSBAND:

And Scheherazade noticed that dawn was approaching and stopped telling her tale. Thereupon [Scheherazade's sister] Dunazade said, "Oh sister, your tale was most wonderful, pleasant, and delightful!"

"It is nothing compared to what I could tell you tomorrow night if the king would spare my life and let me live."

"By Allah," the king thought to himself, "I won't slay her until I hear some more of her wondrous tales."

. . . After this the king got up to perform his official duties, but he did not call upon the vizier to perform the execution. Instead, he went to his assembly hall and began holding court. He judged, appointed, and deposed, forbidding this and permitting that, the rest of the day. After the divan was adjourned, King Shahryar returned to the palace. . . . As [the king and Scheherazade] were relaxing, Dunazade came to her sister and asked her to tell another tale.

"With the king's permission," she said.

And Shahryar replied, "You have my permission."

So Scheherazade resumed her storytelling.

THOUSAND AND ONE NIGHTS

SEE ALSO

- Abbasids
- Arabs
- Entertainment
- Illuminated Manuscripts
- Literature

Timur

THE LAST GREAT CONQUEROR from the steppes of Asia, Timur (1336–1405; also known as Timur Lenk, Tamerlane, and Tamburlaine), in common with Attila the Hun and Genghis Khan, led steppe tribes against the settled civilizations of Asia and created a vast but short-lived empire.

Timur's extraordinary life inspired many later writers, including the sixteenth-century Persian poet Hatifi. This illustration of Timur enthroned is from Hatifi's epic poem Timur-nama.

Rise to Power

Timur was born in Transoxiana (present-day Uzbekistan) into the Barlas tribe, part of a Turko-Mongolian confederation called the Ulus Chagatai. After receiving a wound to the leg while a young man, he gained the nickname Timur Lenk (Timur the Lame). Despite his disability, by around 1360 he had made himself leader of the Barlas.

During the next decade Timur rose to power within the confederation. Since he was not a descendant of Genghis Khan, he could not assume the title of khan (ruler). Instead, he adopted the less exalted title of emir (commander) while exercising effective rule through puppet khans. After marrying into the royal family, he also adopted the title *guregen* (royal son-in-law).

Campaigns

In 1379 Timur began a series of campaigns that would continue, almost without interruption, until his death. Between 1379 and 1387, he conquered eastern Persia (present-day Afghanistan and Iran). He returned to Transoxiana in 1388 to fight off an invasion by the Golden Horde, the Mongol rulers of Russia. After invading the Russian steppes and defeating the Golden Horde in 1391, he expanded his power westward into Iraq. In 1395 he moved north and destroyed the cities of the Golden Horde. His subsequent conquest of northern India culminated in the sack of Delhi in 1398. Campaigning in Anatolia and Syria between 1399 and 1402, he defeated both the Mamluks and the Ottoman Turks.

When Timur was laying siege to Damascus in 1400, the great Arab historian Ibn Khaldun (1332–1406), who was among the besieged, was sent to negotiate. Khaldun later described Timur as "highly intelligent and very perspicacious, addicted

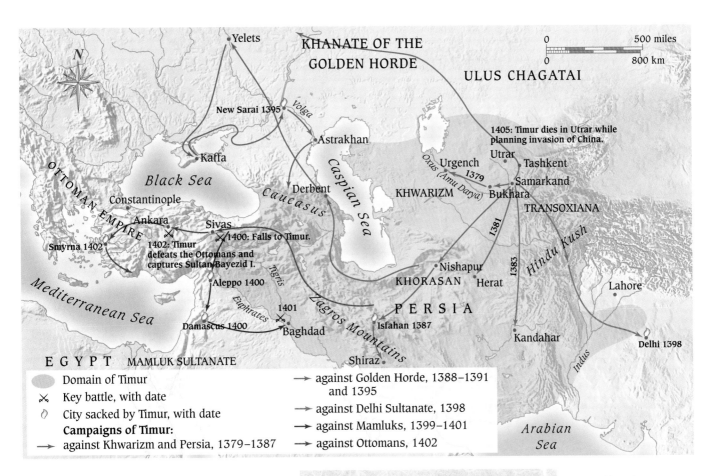

Map showing Timur's campaigns:

- Yelets
- KHANATE OF THE GOLDEN HORDE
- ULUS CHAGATAI
- 0 — 500 miles
- 0 — 800 km
- New Sarai 1395
- _Volga_
- 1405: Timur dies in Utrar while planning invasion of China.
- Utrar
- Urgench 1379
- Tashkent
- Astrakhan
- _Oxus (Amu Darya)_
- Samarkand
- Kaffa
- KHWARIZM
- Bukhara
- _Black Sea_
- Derbent
- _Caspian Sea_
- _Caucasus_
- TRANSOXIANA
- Constantinople
- 1381
- OTTOMAN EMPIRE
- Ankara
- Sivas
- 1400: Falls to Timur.
- 1383
- _Hindu Kush_
- Smyrna 1402
- 1402: Timur defeats the Ottomans and captures Sultan Bayezid I.
- Nishapur
- KHORASAN
- Herat
- Lahore
- Aleppo 1400
- _Tigris_
- _Euphrates_
- _Zagros Mountains_
- PERSIA
- _Mediterranean Sea_
- 1401
- Damascus 1400
- Baghdad
- Isfahan 1387
- Kandahar
- _Indus_
- Delhi 1398
- Shiraz
- EGYPT   MAMLUK SULTANATE
- _Arabian Sea_

Legend:
- Domain of Timur
- ⚔ Key battle, with date
- ◊ City sacked by Timur, with date
- **Campaigns of Timur:**
- → against Khwarizm and Persia, 1379–1387
- → against Golden Horde, 1388–1391 and 1395
- → against Delhi Sultanate, 1398
- → against Mamluks, 1399–1401
- → against Ottomans, 1402

to debate and argument about what he knows and also about what he does not know."

In 1402 Timur won a great victory over the Ottomans at Ankara when he captured Sultan Bayezid I, who had been preparing to attack Constantinople. This victory is thought to have delayed the fall of the Byzantine Empire by half a century. Two years later Timur, half-blind and carried in a litter, set off on his last great campaign—an invasion of China. He reached the city of Utrar, where he died on February 18, 1405.

Rule

Timur appointed sons and grandsons to the governorship of provinces while allowing local rulers to continue in power. He brought craftsmen from all over his empire to his capital, Samarkand, which became a magnificent city. He also encouraged trade

IN 1404 A SPANISH AMBASSADOR VISITED SAMARKAND AND WROTE A DESCRIPTION OF TIMUR:

His Highness . . . commanded us to arise and to stand close up to him that he might the better see us, for his sight was no longer good, indeed he was so infirm and old that his eyelids were falling over his eyes and he could barely raise them to see.

RUY GONZALEZ DE CLAVIJO,
EMBASSY TO TAMERLANE

and agriculture and ruthlessly punished rebellion. In 1401, following an uprising in Baghdad, he destroyed the city and massacred 20,000 citizens.

Although Timur's vast empire fragmented on his death, the Timurid dynasty he established continued to rule large areas of central Asia until the early 1700s.

▲ _Although Timur conquered a vast territory, he was unable to create a lasting empire._

SEE ALSO
- Central Asian Peoples
- Genghis Khan
- Huns

Toltecs

FROM THE NINTH CENTURY through the twelfth, the Toltecs were the dominant power in the area that is now Mexico. In common with the later Aztecs, they created a militaristic society and perhaps sacrificed prisoners of war. From the city of Tula, the Toltecs developed long-distance trade links with settlements throughout Mesoamerica, including the Mayan city of Chichén Itzá. The Aztecs adopted many features of Toltec civilization.

▼ *These so-called Atlantean columns are thought to have held up the roof of a temple in Tula. Each warrior is 15 feet (4.6 m) tall and wears a butterfly-shaped pectoral (breast ornament).*

Origins

The Toltecs emerged following the collapse of the great city of Teotihuacán, which had been the center of the earliest known empire in the region of present-day Mexico. At its height at the beginning of the sixth century, Teotihuacán, which covered more than eight square miles (21 km²), was one of the largest cities in the world.

The destruction of Teotihuacán in the late seventh century marked the beginning of more than two centuries of warfare in Mexico. The region was divided among several small fortified cities, including Tula, founded sometime around 700. The people of Tula, the Toltecs, eventually defeated their rivals, and by 950 they had established themselves as the dominant power in Mexico.

The culture of Teotihuacán was a major influence on the Toltecs, who adopted two gods that were worshiped in the city. One was Tlaloc, the goggle-eyed rain god. The other was a feathered serpent whom the Aztecs would later call Quetzalcoatl (the Toltec name for this god is uncertain).

Tula

The city of Tula covered five square miles (13 km²) and, with around 50,000 people, had a population around a third the size of Teotihuacán's. At the heart of the city was a ceremonial area with two great pyramid temples and two sacred ball courts. There were also Atlantean columns (colossal stone warriors); *chacmools*, sculptures of reclining figures holding a bowl for sacrificial offerings; and a *tzompantli* (skull rack), where the heads of slain enemies were displayed. The temples were decorated with

The Toltecs are thought to have invented the chacmool, a carved reclining figure holding an offering bowl. The close resemblance of this chacmool *from the Mayan city of Chichén Itzá to those found in Tula is taken as evidence of Toltec influence on the Maya.*

carvings of jaguars and eagles eating human hearts, images that have been interpreted by some historians as symbols of human sacrifice. (The Aztecs would later go into battle dressed as eagles and jaguars and would sacrifice prisoners by cutting their heart out.)

Trade

Archaeologists digging in Tula have discovered pottery and obsidian from other parts of Mesoamerica. Further evidence of long-distance trade has been found in the city of Chichén Itzá, in the Mayan heartland of Yucatán, some nine hundred miles (1,500 km) to the east of Tula. Despite the distance between the two cities, there are striking similarities between them. The *chacmools* and colonnaded halls found in both Tula and Chichén Itzá were otherwise extremely rare in Mesoamerica at this time.

Owing to these and other similarities, archaeologists used to believe that Chichén Itzá was a Toltec outpost. However, it is now generally believed that the Mayan rulers of Chichén Itzá adopted aspects of Toltec culture as a result of trading and political alliances.

EVIDENCE OF THE TOLTECS

Knowledge of the Toltecs derives from two sources: from the archaeological study of Tula and other sites and from Toltec traditions that were preserved by the Aztecs and later written down by Spanish friars. The problem for historians is that the two sources of information are contradictory. The Aztecs saw the Toltecs as a superhuman people who invented all the arts and crafts and conquered a great empire that extended across Mexico from coast to coast. Yet the small size of Tula suggests that its people lacked the resources for such expansion. Most historians doubt that a true Toltec empire existed.

▼ *This shell mosaic work may represent a warrior wearing a helmet in the shape of an animal—either a coyote or a bat—or Quetzalcoatl rising from the jaws of the earth.*

palace was burned down. The city was abandoned until the rise of the Aztecs in the fourteenth century, when it was partially reoccupied.

Tula was regarded as a sacred site by the Aztecs, whose emperors claimed to be of Toltec descent, probably in order to legitimize their own rule. When the Aztecs planned the ceremonial areas of their own cities, they copied the layout of Tula. The last Aztec emperor, Montezuma II, sent parties to Tula to dig for precious relics, which were then brought back to his own city, Tenochtitlán, and placed in the temple.

Relics for the Aztecs

Around 1200, Tula was destroyed (by whom is not known). All but one of the *chacmools* were decapitated, and the main

SEE ALSO
• Aztecs • Maya

CHRONOLOGY

c. 500
The city of Teotihuacán is at the height of its power and prosperity.

c. 700
Teotihuacán is destroyed; Tula is founded.

c. 800
Tula's growth continues.

c. 950
Tula becomes the most powerful city in the region (present-day Mexico).

c. 990
Toltec influence begins to be felt at Chichén Itzá, nine hundred miles to the east of Tula.

c. 1200
Tula is destroyed.

Tools and Technology

TECHNOLOGICAL DEVELOPMENT began in prehistoric times, when people first used sticks, sharp-edged stones, and other simple tools. During the Middle Ages people in some areas of the world were still using primitive tools. In China and, later, Europe people began to develop highly sophisticated tools and technologies. By the later Middle Ages enthusiasm for technological innovation was widespread in Europe.

◀ *This illumination, from a thirteenth-century manuscript describing the life of Saint George, depicts a farmer using oxen to pull a plow fitted with an iron plowshare.*

The most important technological developments in medieval Europe were in the fields of agriculture, metalworking, and cloth making. With a heavy iron-wheeled plow, introduced from the sixth century, the cultivation of deforested land could keep pace with the demand for food of a growing population.

Wheeled plows and carts were pulled first by oxen and later by horses. With improvements made to harnesses and collars between the sixth and ninth centuries, a horse could pull a heavier load. Around 900, after the reinvention of the iron horseshoe (first used in ancient Rome), horses rapidly took over from oxen as beasts of burden.

The increased availability of iron in Europe from the eighth century improved the quality of plows and other tools. Tools for agriculture, carpentry, stonemasonry, and building were made from wrought iron hammered by a blacksmith. Cast iron, stronger than wrought iron, became available in Europe from around 1350, when the first blast furnace was built in Sweden.

Making cloth was a laborious process at the beginning of the Middle Ages. Individual threads were spun by hand from a mass of wool, cotton, or flax and then woven on a vertical loom. Cloth making in Europe was greatly speeded up in the eleventh century, when a horizontal loom, worked with a foot treadle, was introduced

Chinese papermaker was captured in 751. Papermaking arrived in Europe in the tenth century, when it was introduced to Muslim Spain and Sicily. The Chinese developed woodblock printing in the seventh century and movable clay type in the eleventh century. Movable metal type was first used in Korea in the fifteenth century.

Two Chinese developments revolutionized warfare. The stirrup, developed by the Chinese from an Indian idea, had reached Iran by 694 and was adopted by the Franks around 730. Stirrups greatly increased the military importance of mounted soldiers; large-scale battles were fought from horseback for the first time. The Chinese used gunpowder for fireworks, bombs, and grenades from the eleventh century. Gunpowder reached Europe in 1268, and by the mid-fourteenth century it had changed warfare forever.

Water

The Chinese first used dikes to limit flood damage and irrigation systems to water land before the Middle Ages. In 1126 monks in Artois, in northern France, drilled the first artesian well—one from which water springs under natural pressure without the need for a pump. Systems of irrigation canals, built in northern Italy from the twelfth century, were used to grow crops imported from India, such as rice and cotton.

Flowing river water drove water mills, which were used all over Europe throughout the Middle Ages. In 1044 tidal mills appeared in Venice. Mills, used at first to grind corn, were adopted by beer makers in eighth-century France and spread rapidly to other industries. By the eleventh century mills were being used to drive bellows and hammers in forges.

from China. Another important innovation, the spinning wheel, was invented around 1280.

Chinese Inventions

Numerous medieval innovations originated in China. Increased traffic along the Silk Road, a network of trade routes that ran west from China to the borders of Europe, as well as sea trade between Muslim nations and the East, aided the spread of Chinese knowledge and technologies.

The Chinese had used cast iron since the third century BCE and already had heavy plows by the beginning of the Middle Ages. Paper and printing were first developed in China. Paper, used in China before the first century CE, was adopted in Japan, Korea, and India in the early Middle Ages. A paper mill was created in Baghdad after a

Machine Making

The crank, in use in China under the Han dynasty (206 BCE–220 CE), first appeared in Europe around 830 near Reims, in northeastern France. A device that converts linear movement into circular movement, the crank was the basis of numerous types of machines, including many drawn by the French architect Villard de Honnecourt (c. 1225–c. 1250). The first compound crank was used in a brace and bit (a type of drill) made around 1420 in Flanders.

There was widespread enthusiasm for engineering in medieval Europe. More ambitious projects included Eilmer of Malmesbury's glider, which flew six hundred feet (200 m) in 1010. Few of the complex machines sketched by Leonardo da Vinci (1452–1519) could be made at the time. Despite the limitations of contemporary technology, da Vinci's sketches demonstrate his understanding and appreciation of sophisticated engineering.

▲ *This flying machine, sketched by Leonardo da Vinci, has a screw that enables it to take off and land vertically—much like a modern helicopter. Leonardo also sketched a submarine, a parachute, and a bicycle.*

THE MAGNETIC COMPASS

Primitive compasses had been used in China since 200 BCE. A modern style of compass, with a magnetized needle floating on water or suspended by a silk thread, appeared in the eighth century. The Chinese used compasses for navigation from the eleventh century. The first recorded use of the compass in the Mediterranean dates from around 1180. Whether Mediterannean sailors invented the compass independently or learned about it from the Chinese is not known.

SEE ALSO
- Astronomy
- Calendars and Clocks
- Guilds
- Mining and Metalworking
- Printing
- Transportation
- Warfare
- Waterways

Torture

TORTURE, THE INFLICTION or threat of intense pain or humiliation, has generally been used to extract information or a criminal confession from a prisoner or to coerce a prisoner into a given course of action (the word comes from the Latin *torquere*, "to twist"). Torture has been linked with political policy and the dictates of religious ritual. In some cultures the practice of torture was challenged on grounds of either morality or efficacy—for then as now, information gained by torture was frequently unreliable.

The Americas

In the Americas torture was practiced as part of sacred rituals. Late-eighth-century Mayan wall paintings depict tortured captives with blood spouting from their fingertips. In the fifteenth century the Aztecs regarded flaying (skinning alive) and live human sacrifice as a religious duty. Among native North American peoples, torture was a ritual of vengeance. Selected enemy captives might be tortured for days on end by each social group within the tribe. A prisoner's fingernails might be pulled out or his limbs bound with thongs, or he might be forced to walk on red-hot embers.

Europe

Legally authorized torture took many forms in the Roman Empire, from extreme corporal punishment to forms of capital punishment, such as crucifixion, in which the victim died a slow death. Roman law—and with it the legal sanction for torture—survived into the Middle Ages in the Byzantine Empire and parts of southern Europe. Although rare in the early Middle Ages, judicial torture became increasingly common from the fourteenth century onward.

Northern European judicial and legal systems allowed for the violent treatment of criminal suspects through such practices as trial by combat and trial by ordeal, whose outcome was, it was deemed, decided by God. Although outright torture was not sanctioned by English common law, special

▼ *This late-eighth-century wall painting from Bonampak, Mexico, shows captives with their fingernails pulled out being brought before a Mayan lord.*

licenses for torture were issued by Henry II (reigned 1154–1189) and other English kings. It was also common for troops in the field to torture their captives.

Torture and Religion

Although some medieval churchmen criticized torture, in some instances Christian authorities condoned it. The Byzantine emperor Justinian I, who ruled from 527, decreed that anyone who insulted a priest in church should be tortured. In 1252 Pope Innocent IV ordered the torture of heretics, (those whose religious beliefs were at odds with official doctrine). The Spanish Inquisition, a religious court, was founded in 1478. Under a monk named Tomás de Torquemada (1420–1498), the Inquisition became infamous for the torture of heretics (modern historians consider this reputation very exaggerated).

Methods of Torture

The duke of Exeter, the constable of the Tower of London from 1420, introduced a rack, a frame on which the body was slowly

TORTURE OF THE TEMPLARS

The French king Philip IV (reigned 1268–1314) coveted the wealth of the Templars, a religious order of knights. In 1310 Philip arrested all Templars, accused them of immorality, and sought suppression of their order by the pope. To gain confessions, Philip's torturers starved the captives, deprived them of sleep, humiliated them, tied them to triangular frames and then dropped and jolted them, and burned the soles of their feet. Those who confessed were burned alive.

stretched. Known as "the duke of Exeter's daughter," the rack left its victims crippled or dead from suffocation. Other methods of torture developed in Europe included crushing the body with weights or spikes, breaking teeth, screwing thumbs, extreme confinement in an iron cage, hanging by the wrists, flogging, and beating.

This thirteenth-century manuscript illustration depicts the torture and martyrdom of Saint Margaret of Antioch, a third-century martyr.

SEE ALSO

- Captivity and Ransom
- Crime and Punishment
- Heresy

Tournaments

THE TOURNAMENT, a form of structured military training as well as an entertaining spectacle, probably developed among European knights during the twelfth century. The name *tournament* (literally, "turning") may refer to the coordinated circling motion of a group of riders.

Early tournaments, or tourneys, were fought with sharp weapons over huge areas of countryside. Fortunes could be won and lost, since a captured opponent had to give up horse and armor or pay for his release.

During the thirteenth century the size of the fighting area (known as the lists) gradually decreased. A new form of combat, the joust—a single contest between two mounted opponents—became popular. A knight scored points for unhorsing an opponent or handling his lance well. A jousting knight could show off his skills without being attacked by several opponents at once.

Playing It Safe

In order to reduce casualties, blunted weapons were introduced. Though jousts of war continued to require participants to carry sharp weapons, in jousts of peace, lances were blunted or fitted with a coronel, a ring of small points that spread the force of a blow. These and other such weapons were called arms of courtesy.

Safer armor was also developed, especially for jousts of peace. One example was the frog-mouthed helm, a helmet whose narrow eye slit had a lower edge that jutted forward to protect the eyes from lance points or fragments of a shattered shaft.

Types of Tournaments

A *behourd* was a less formal event, while round tables, complete with jousts, were held, especially in England, to relive the legendary glory of Arthurian times. The presence of ladies also became important, both for the encouragement of contestants and for the presentation of prizes.

In the fourteenth century foot combat became increasingly popular at tournaments. Two opponents often fought with poleaxes, with the numbers of blows landed carefully watched by the judges. More and more rules were introduced to control tournaments, and shows were carefully planned. Specially appointed heralds carried challenges from court to court.

From the fifteenth century the tilt, a barrier to separate jousters and prevent col-

AN ACCOUNT OF A 1443 JOUST BETWEEN JEHAN DE COMPAYS AND THE ESQUIRE ANTHOINE DE VAUDREY AT A TOURNAMENT HELD NEAR DIJON, IN BURGUNDY:

The eighth, ninth and tenth encounters were barren, but at the eleventh, and last, de Vaudrey broke his lance upon the shield of de Compays. Thus was the combat finished, and they were brought before the Duke, who, however, did not tell them to shake hands, for they still had to fight one another on foot, according to the significance of the violet shield, . . . which had been touched by Savoy the Herald at the request of the said de Compays.

OLIVIER DE LA MARCHE

lisions, came into use. The lavish *pas d'armes*, seen especially in Burgundy, involved one or more fighters holding a piece of ground against all comers. The *pas d'armes* was often the scene for the reenactment of legends. A version of the tourney appeared in which the teams used blunt swords and clubs and wore helmets with a grill at the front.

In the twelfth and thirteenth centuries tournaments were often declared illegal by kings. The early tournament was seen sometimes (not without cause) as a potential hotbed of sedition and an occasion for the treasonous mustering of troops. Nevertheless, tournaments retained their popularity into the seventeenth century, when they were replaced by carousels, peaceful displays of horsemanship.

SEE ALSO
- **Arms and Armor** • **Cavalry** • **Chivalry**
- **Entertainment** • **Knights** • **Warfare**

▼ *A 1470 French illustration of knights in frog-mouthed helms jousting over a barrier.*

Trade

IMPROVEMENTS IN METHODS of production from the early Middle Ages brought about great increases in local and regional trade throughout Europe. Surplus food and goods were sold for money or exchanged for other goods. International trade grew up as roads and communications improved. Trade routes linked East Asia with western Europe by both land and sea.

Patterns of Trade

With improvements in agricultural and manufacturing technologies in Europe from the early Middle Ages, many local industries generated surplus produce that could be traded locally or farther afield. The kind of goods that a given region could produce was determined by natural factors, such as climate, soil type, and the raw materials available. For instance, a coastal village might trade fish with an inland town that produced wool. Mines in central Europe produced metals that were traded for goods that central Europeans did not produce—fruit and cloth, for example.

Merchants and Bankers

An emerging class of middlemen did not produce goods themselves but acted as merchants. They bought goods from suppliers and sold them at a profit. From the thirteenth century, bankers, based mostly in Italy, Germany, and Flanders, financed trading expeditions. By the end of the Middle Ages, bankers were gaining political power, particularly in Italy.

▼ *In this fourteenth-century miniature from the Drapers' Guild's Book of Statutes, an Italian cloth merchant displays a sample of cloth to prospective customers.*

At the center of this fifteenth-century French manuscript illustration are two cloth merchants, their wares displayed on a stall in front of them.

Markets and Trade Routes

The number of trade fairs and markets increased rapidly in medieval Europe. Initially, a king or local ruler supervised local markets and fairs and imposed taxes on those who held and attended them. Markets were tightly controlled, first by the lords and later by town authorities and the guilds and corporations, which wanted to protect their own traders. Between centers of production, local and international trade routes emerged. Along the routes inns and hostelries provided accommodation and sustenance for traveling merchants.

European Trade

From the sixth century to the tenth, pagan Slavs from central Europe, many of them prisoners of war, were sold as slaves to the Muslim traders of North Africa and Spain. This slave trade stopped when the Slavic countries were Christianized.

From the ninth century traders from eastern Europe and Russia (including present-day Ukraine) carried furs, timber, fish, and metals to western Europe and to Constantinople (present-day Istanbul) and other eastern trading posts. Traveling along the Volkhov River from the north, these traders passed through the important town of Novgorod. Metals mined in southern and central Germany were carried across the Alps and traded in Italy.

The Hanseatic League

From the middle of the twelfth century, merchants in northern European and Baltic cities began to form societies called Hansas. The Hansas promoted trade with foreign cities and set up trade agreements for their members. As Hansas from different cities joined together, a network called the Hanseatic League developed.

The Hanseatic League became a powerful organization of one hundred cities in the Holy Roman Empire. Trading posts were built throughout the Baltic region, and towns were established where there

THE WOOL TRADE

English wool, renowned as the best in Europe, was sold in Flanders, where it was made into cloth that was then sold to Italy. Italian artisans used dyes from the East to make finished fabrics that were sold around Europe.

At first, the wool trade was conducted overland, often through the great trade fairs in Champagne, a region of northeastern France. Later, wool was transported around Europe by sea. As a result, French trade fairs declined from the fourteenth century. When the English began to weave the wool into cloth and sell directly to Italian buyers, Flemish involvement in the trade changed to brokering and banking.

had been none. From northern Germany the league ran ships around the Baltic Sea and sometimes as far south as the Bay of Biscay. Hanseatic traders carried fish, timber, furs, metal, and mineral ores to exchange for wine, fruit, and salt from the south. The league controlled maritime trade in northern Europe and had numerous monopolies until its collapse in the sixteenth century.

Trade with the East

The two-way trade of goods between the Far East and Europe was established by the seventh century. Asian spices and silks were brought to Europe, and European grain, oil, wine, fruit, metals, glass, timber, salt, and textiles were exported to the East. Goods were transported by land along the Silk Road, a network of trade routes that crossed central Asia, or by sea through the Persian Gulf and across the Indian Ocean.

Land and sea routes between Europe and Asia were controlled by Arabs for much of the Middle Ages. Arab traders loaded goods onto their ships in the ports of China and India and transferred them onto European galleys upon reaching the eastern end of the Mediterranean.

The European centers of trade with the East were the Italian cities of Genoa and Venice and the Byzantine capital, Constantinople. Around the Genoese-controlled Russian port of Azov and the ports of the Black Sea, goods from western Europe, the East, and Russia converged.

▲ *This depiction of the Aragonese fleet arriving at the busy Italian port of Naples is part of the renowned fifteenth-century* Tavola Strozzi, *the earliest-known representation of the city.*

SEE ALSO

- Agriculture • Cities and Towns • Guilds
- Manufacturing • Money
- Ships and Seafaring • Silk Road
- Taxes and Tithes • Transportation

Transportation

THE MIDDLE AGES saw improvements in the breeding and equipping of horses, the widespread adoption of horseshoes and stirrups, and improved harnesses for horses and oxen. Wheeled vehicles, however, were generally primitive and of limited use, and advances in land transport were limited by the poor condition of roads.

le nel uoles prendre a celer ne bous quier
amiral bous deffie z tuit fi chenalier

European Roads

The Roman Empire had possessed a first-rate road network. The long, straight Roman highways were carefully surveyed and well constructed. However, the political fragmentation that accompanied the collapse of the Western Roman Empire in 476 led to a decline in civil administration. The Roman roads fell into neglect.

Roads in medieval Europe were deeply potholed and mired in mud for much of the year. It was far quicker to transport freight by river. Another obstacle to road development was robbery. In 1285 an English statute ordered that broad spaces be cleared on both sides of a road in order to prevent travelers from being ambushed.

Horses in Europe

The chief means of transport was the horse. In the early Middle Ages stocky ponies carried soldiers to war and farmers to market. In the later Middle Ages larger horses, such as palfreys (fine riding horses) and destriers (huge warhorses), were bred for knights. Most people traveled around on workaday riding horses (called hackneys or nags). A single horse often carried two

This fourteenth-century manuscript illustration depicts a wheeled cart, drawn by two horses, carrying barrels, shields, and a soldier.

riders. Goods were carried in panniers or saddlebags on packhorses (known as sumpters). Donkeys were also commonly used for riding and for carrying goods, especially in southern Europe.

Heavy loads were hauled on wagons by teams of oxen. Only farmers and peasants or, more notoriously, prisoners bound for the gallows rode in a cart. Peoples of Europe's icy far north crossed the snow on wooden sleds pulled by horses.

Travel in Asia

The people of the Asian steppes had perfected the art of horse breeding. The stunning military successes of the Mongols and other steppe peoples was due largely to the durability and speed of their mounts.

Packhorses and Bactrian camels (two-humped camels) transported goods along the Silk Road, the network of trade routes that led west from China. Merchants traveled in armed groups called caravans in order to protect themselves from attack by bandits. In South and East Asia domesticated elephants were used to haul timber, as well as for ceremonial processions.

China had the most advanced transportation system in the world. A noble might travel in a horse-drawn cart or a litter (a curtained couch carried in the manner of a stretcher). Goods were transported by ox wagon or donkey cart or hauled or pushed by hand in a sturdy wheelbarrow—a Chinese invention also adapted to carry passengers.

Chinese workers maintained and extended roads and built bridges over the new canals. The Venetian traveler Marco Polo, who arrived in China in 1275, reported that the city of Suzhou alone had six thousand bridges.

Across the Sahara

In sub-Saharan Africa canoes plied rivers and lakes. Dhows (Arab sailing boats with a triangular sail) served East African ports. North African peoples traveled on horses, donkeys, and dromedaries (one-humped camels) and in wheeled carts. The dromedary greatly boosted trans-Saharan trade in the third century CE, and indigenous kingdoms rose up in West Africa. The rulers of these kingdoms imported Arabian horses.

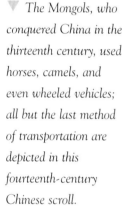

▼ *The Mongols, who conquered China in the thirteenth century, used horses, camels, and even wheeled vehicles; all but the last method of transportation are depicted in this fourteenth-century Chinese scroll.*

THE CHAR

By the fourteenth century European ladies of the court might travel in a char, an early form of coach. The char had a long wooden base; four high, spoked wheels; paneled sides; and a hooped canopy of elaborately painted canvas. A char could be drawn by a team of five horses. The poor state of the roads made the char lurch and rock, and it was not until the sixteenth and seventeenth centuries that shock-absorbing springs began to make coach travel more bearable.

Ibn Battutah

One of the most determined travelers of the Middle Ages was Ibn Battutah (1304–c. 1368), a Moroccan. From 1325 to 1354, Battutah visited places as far apart as Spain, Arabia, Bukhara (in present-day Uzbekistan), Sumatra (Indonesia), and China. He also crossed the Sahara Desert to the remote trading post of Tombouctou. On land Battutah traveled by camel, horse, mule, and oxcart. His watergoing vessels included a raft, a dhow, and a junk (a Chinese sailing vessel).

Lands without the Wheel

The Aztecs, Incas, and other peoples of the Americas had canoes and oceangoing rafts —but no wheel before the arrival of Europeans. In view of their technological advances, the absence of wheeled vehicles might seem extraordinary. However, there were no native animals suitable for hauling carts. People traveled across the Incan Empire by foot or by litter. Produce was carried by porters or on the back of llamas. The Incan Empire was linked by paved roads and rope bridges. Official messages were carried by teams of runners from one relay station to the next.

There was no wheeled transport in medieval Oceania. Australia, in common with the Americas, lacked suitable animals. Australian aborigines, following traditional routes and landmarks, covered vast distances on foot. Peoples of the small islands of the Pacific crossed thousands of miles of ocean by canoe.

SEE ALSO
- **Africa**
- **Agriculture**
- **Aztecs**
- **China**
- **Exploration**
- **Incas**
- **Ships and Seafaring**
- **Silk Road**
- **Trade**

Umayyads

THE UMAYYADS (661–750) were the first dynasty to rule the Islamic Empire. At its height the Umayyad Empire extended from India in the east to Spain in the west and encompassed northern Africa and the Middle East. After the fall of the Umayyads in Syria in 750, members of the dynasty established the emirate of Córdoba in Spain, which survived until 1031.

The first Muslim civil war (656–661) arose out of a struggle for the office of caliph, the spiritual and political ruler of all Muslims. Muawiyah (c. 602–680), the governor of Syria, was victorious; in 661 he became the first caliph of the Umayyad dynasty. Muawiyah conquered Egypt and the central Asian province of Khorasan and invaded northwestern Africa.

In the lands they conquered, the Muslim Arabs segregated themselves from their subject peoples. Whereas the previous method of choosing the caliph had been election (at least in theory), Muawiyah introduced the practice of hereditary succession. Upon his death his son Yazid (reigned 680–683) became caliph.

Conflict under Yazid

Many Muslims, both Arabs and non-Arabs, disagreed with the Umayyad line of succession, believing instead that the new ruler should be a descendant of the prophet Muhammad, the founder of Islam. Early opponents of the Umayyads supported Husayn, the son of Muhammad's son-in-

▶ *The courtyard of the Great Mosque of Damascus, which was built between 705 and 715 by the Umayyad caliph al-Walid I.*

law Ali. Husayn's attempt to seize the caliphate was thwarted when Yazid defeated him at the Battle of Karbala (681).

Challenges

There was frequent religious debate about whether the Umayyads were practicing Islam correctly. Members of the Umayyad court lived in luxury while many of their subjects lived in poverty. The dynasty was subject to continual challenges. In western Arabia in the 680s, the Umayyads faced a rebellion by those who wanted a return to the egalitarian ideals of the earliest days of Islam. The Shias, who argued for the right of Ali and his descendants to succeed to the caliphate, rose up against the Umayyads to avenge Husayn's death. Another rebellion was led by the Kharijites, a Muslim sect whose members held that the caliph should be elected by all Muslims. The Umayyads finally quashed these uprisings in 691.

Peak and Decline

The peak of Umayyad power was reached under Abd al-Malik (685–705) and his son, al-Walid (705–715). Arabic became the official language throughout the empire, Arabs replaced local officials in positions of power, and a new Arabic coinage was introduced. The first great Islamic monument, the Dome of the Rock, was completed in Jerusalem in 691. The strict rules that formerly isolated Muslims from the empire's subject peoples were now relaxed.

Al-Walid further expanded Islamic territory. In the West he continued the conquest of North Africa and in 711 set up a kingdom in Spain. In the East he conquered Bukhara and Samarkand (in present-day Uzbekistan) in 715. However, the tide began to turn when the Byzantine emperor Leo III defeated the Syrian army in 717.

HASAN, HUSAYN'S BROTHER AND A GRANDSON OF MUHAMMAD, WROTE A LETTER TO MUAWIYAH UPON BEING FORCED TO GIVE UP HIS CLAIMS TO THE CALIPHATE:

You, oh Muawiyah, are trying to take an authority you do not deserve. You do not possess any known merit in religion. . . . So give up your persistence in falsehood, for you are certainly aware that I am far more entitled to the caliphate than you in the eyes of God and all worthy people.

QUOTED BY THE SHIA HISTORIAN AL-ISFAHANI

▲ A page from a Koran, the holy book of Islam, made in Bukhara—a city first brought into the Islamic Empire by the Umayyads in 715.

After Leo's victory the Umayyad dynasty went into decline. Under Umar II (717–720) the caliphate suffered a financial crisis, and feuds broke out between the Kalb and Qays, two Arab tribes.

Hisham (724–743) arrested the decline to some extent, but after his death the feuds between the Kalb and Qays erupted into major revolts. Religious opposition from Kharijite and Shia groups gathered force. Kharijites and Shiites assisted the rival Abbasids, who defeated the Umayyad ruler Marwan II in 750.

Afangge font annez cemeſt ins.

Dauāt lirois marſille aune ione dis.
O ela reſpoiſe azles ozantnāt leſreais.
Jlloz reſpōnet reluī auōs apzis.

▲ *A fourteenth-century historical manuscript illustration of the emir of Córdoba. Following the unrest of the eleventh century, the petty Muslim kingdoms fought over Córdoba, which was eventually conquered by the Castilians in 1236 and became part of Christian Spain.*

Córdoba

The Abbasids killed every Umayyad they could capture. However, one Umayyad, Abd ar-Rahman, escaped to Spain, where he defeated the governor of al-Andalus (the Arabs' name for the Iberian peninsula) in 756 and made himself emir, with Córdoba as his capital.

In Córdoba, Abd ar-Rahman instituted the Umayyad system of rule and repelled attacks from Charlemagne and Abbasid caliphs and rebellions by Muslims and Berbers. Under his rule Córdoba became a great center of culture and learning.

The peak of the emirate was attained under Abd ar-Rahman III (ruled 929–961), who expanded Umayyad territory and declared himself caliph. In the early

eleventh century there was great political unrest, and in 1031 al-Andalus split into numerous independent kingdoms.

THE UMAYYAD CALIPHS

661–680	Muawiyah I
680–683	Yazid I
683–684	Muawiyah II
684–685	Marwan I
685–705	Abd al-Malik
705–715	al-Walid I
715–717	Sulayman
717–720	Umar II
720–724	Yazid II
724–743	Hisham ibn Abd al-Malik
743–744	al-Walid II
744	Yazid III
744	Ibrahim ibn al-Walid
744–750	Marwan II

CHRONOLOGY

661
Muawiyah establishes the Umayyad dynasty.

681
Yazid defeats Husayn at Karbala.

680s
Umayyads face numerous rebellions.

691
The Dome of the Rock mosque is completed in Jerusalem.

711
Al-Walid I establishes Muslim rule in Spain.

715
Conquers Bukhara and Samarkand.

717
The Syrian army is defeated by Leo III.

750
The Abbasids defeat the Umayyads.

756
Abd ar-Rahman becomes emir of Córdoba.

1031
Umayyad rule in Spain ends.

Universities

IN 1221 TEACHERS AND STUDENTS in Paris first used the Latin word *universitas* (which denotes an independent corporation or society) to describe their scholarly group. The university system grew rapidly during the later Middle Ages. New institutions for higher learning, attracting students from all over Europe, evolved in many countries across the continent.

Origins of the Universities

The University of Paris and the other early universities came into being in much the same way as the trade guilds. Students and masters (the name given to more experienced scholars) began to form organized study groups. Eventually these groups were given charters that formally recognized their special status and gave them legal control over their student members.

Several factors contributed to the rise of universities. The cathedral schools had established the importance of formal advanced education. The rediscovery of ancient philosophical texts generated a new enthusiasm for learning. The development of new teaching methods made learning more attractive. Teachers began employing dialectic, a classical method of using logic to elicit truth by pursuing a false argument until its contradictory nature is exposed. Finally, the reputation of certain important teachers, notably Peter Abelard, gave fame to particular centers of learning. By attracting more students, these centers developed into universities.

University Life

University studies generally began in late September or early October. Students would usually gather in churches, since universities did not possess their own buildings. Students were often taxed or charged fees, but care was taken to ensure that poor

In this illustration to a fifteenth-century French manuscript, a master (center) conducts a lesson in theology at the Sorbonne, one of the colleges that is part of the University of Paris.

All Souls College, pictured here, was founded as part of Oxford University in 1438. Colleges were created by wealthy benefactors who wanted to provide a place where poor students could live.

students would receive financial support. Some schools required that masters be paid, while at others masters were supported by gifts, the government, or the church.

Study followed a basic pattern. First, a master would lecture the students, generally about a text. The master would offer basic background information and then add his own views on the significance of the subject. The lectures were followed by formal debates and discussions in which the students were required to prove their knowledge, offer their own conclusions, and defend their views.

Students had to complete a rigorous program of lectures and discussions. All students began studying with the master of arts, who taught logic and debating skills. After completing these studies, a student could work with a master of a more advanced field, such as theology, law, or medicine. These advanced studies, especially in theology, often gave rise to controversies and debates that sometimes spread to other universities or even had an impact on the church.

The Spread of Universities

The two main types of universities were based on the models of Paris and Bologna (in Italy). At Paris the masters held the power and determined how the institution would be run. Most northern European universities followed the Parisian pattern. Bologna, founded in the eleventh century, provided a different model. Students at Bologna, unlike their Parisian counterparts, paid fees to support their masters. At Bologna students could threaten to withhold payment until the masters made policy decisions with which they agreed. Much of the power at Bologna thus rested in the hands of the students.

While the universities of Paris and Bologna came into being through a process of evolution, others were founded, often by popes and rulers. Over time, such institutions appeared in England, Scotland, Germany, Scandinavia, the Low Countries, Spain, Portugal, Hungary, and Poland. Certain universities gained fame for expertise in specific subject areas. The arts and theology faculties at Paris were highly rated, whereas Bologna was known as a center of legal studies. Oxford University, in England, was famous for its teaching in theology and canon law (church law). The university at Salamanca, Spain, was another center of theology. Montpellier, in southern France, was renowned for the quality of its medical education.

PETER ABELARD c. 1079–1144

Peter Abelard studied first in Anjou and then in Paris. After disagreements with his teachers, he left to become a teacher himself. In 1113 Abelard moved to the cathedral school of Notre-Dame, where he began applying his skills in philosophy and debating to theological studies. Soon after, Abelard was hired to tutor a young woman named Héloïse. When the pair fell in love and had a child, Heloïse's uncle—who had hired Abelard in the first place—was outraged. Around 1118 the uncle sent two men to attack and maim Abelard.

Abelard then entered the prominent abbey of Saint-Denis. He continued writing and engaging in theological debate. In 1121 he was condemned for heresy. The next year he left Saint-Denis to found a new chapel. Students soon flocked to him, and he began teaching again. Abelard eventually established a convent for a group of nuns, led by Héloïse. The two lovers were buried together.

Byzantine Education

The education system of the Byzantine Empire operated on a much smaller scale than that of western Europe. Education at Byzantine schools was less dominated by religion; instead, universities focused on preparing administrators to work for the empire. Higher education in the Byzantine Empire was provided mainly by private teachers. Although organized groups of teachers did emerge, especially in Constantinople, they were not part of an official institution or corporation.

◄ *Abelard (left) teaches Héloïse in this illustration from a fourteenth-century manuscript of* The Romance of the Rose. *Their tragic tale is one of the best-known love stories of the Middle Ages.*

SEE ALSO

- Churches and Cathedrals
- Cities and Towns
- Education
- Guilds

Vandals

A GERMANIC PEOPLE of Scandinavian or Baltic origin, the Vandals migrated south and settled in parts of modern-day Poland and around the Carpathian Mountains. They remained there for three hundred years. Around 400 CE they moved west and south to Spain and Africa, where they engaged the forces of the weakened Roman Empire. In 533 the Byzantine general Belisarius comprehensively defeated the Vandals.

Saint Nicasius is depicted bowing before a group of Vandals in this carving, which is mounted on the exterior of the Church of Saint-Nicaise in Reims, in northeastern France. Nicasius, who was the archbishop of Reims, was martyred in 453.

The Vandals settled in eastern Europe sometime between the first century and the late fourth century. Around 370 the Huns swept west from their central Asian homeland. Rather than try to resist the fearsome Huns, the Vandals uprooted and moved west.

Rome's frontier defenses were weak, and in 406 the Vandals easily crossed the Rhine River into western Europe. After fighting through Gaul and sacking several cities in the process, they crossed the Pyrenees into Spain in 409.

The Vandals settled throughout the Iberian Peninsula. In 416 the Visigoths, who were based in the Gaulish province of Aquitaine, attacked the Vandals on behalf of the Roman Empire. The Visigoths virtually eliminated one group of Vandals and their allies. The survivors moved to southern Spain. In 425 King Gunderic led the Vandals in a conquest of the Roman cities of Cartagena and Seville. However, the Visigoths continued to exert such pressure on the Vandals that the Vandals turned their attention to North Africa.

Conflicts with Rome

The Roman Empire in North Africa, though prosperous, was subject to revolts by native peoples and simmering discontent over high taxes. In 429 the Vandals, led by

Gunderic's brother and heir Genseric, crossed the Mediterranean in captured Roman ships. In Africa they faced little opposition, except at Carthage and Hippo. The Vandals had gained control of much of North Africa by 431, when they defeated two major Roman armies.

The Vandal conquests were a serious threat to Rome, which depended on North African grain. In 435 Rome offered the Vandals a treaty that granted them power over North Africa on condition that the area remain part of the Roman Empire. Genseric accepted.

Rise and Fall

Taking full advantage of the new treaty, Genseric prepared to attack Sicily. After the Vandals took Palermo and the stronghold of Lilybaeum, Rome offered a new treaty in 442, one that granted the Vandals greater control over the best lands in North Africa.

In 455, when an important Roman general and the emperor were both murdered, Genseric brought the Vandals to Rome. Ignoring the pope's plea to spare the city, he spent two weeks plundering it. The Vandals next captured Corsica, Sardinia, and other Mediterranean islands. In 476 they were granted the Mediterranean islands and Africa by treaty.

▲ *Flavius Stilicho (left), a general of mixed Roman and Vandal stock, married Serena (right), the daughter of a Roman emperor. Rumors that he planned to seize the throne led to his execution and that of his son Eucherius (center).*

The Vandals remained powerful until 533, when the Byzantine emperor Justinian sent a large army under the general Belisarius. Weakened by internal revolts and poor leadership, the Vandals were easily overcome. They were absorbed into the empire and lost their distinct identity.

SOCIETY AND CULTURE

The Vandals are best known for their military exploits; relatively little evidence survives of their society and culture. Contemporary reports describe them as tall, fair-skinned, and blond. Authority was concentrated in the king, especially in times of war. While in Spain they converted to Arianism, a heretical form of Christianity. Archaeological evidence found in North Africa suggests that the Vandals lived quite luxuriously. They had rich buildings, amphitheaters, public baths, gardens, fountains, statues, and paintings. Very few writings by Vandals survive. The modern English word *vandal* is a testament to the Vandals' destructive power.

SEE ALSO
- Belisarius
- Byzantine Empire
- Huns
- Rome
- Visigothic Spain

Venice

THE CITY OF VENICE straddles a group of islands in a lagoon on Italy's northeastern coast. During the Middle Ages, Venice, then a city-state, became one of the foremost powers in Europe. Venetian might was founded on the city's naval supremacy and control of Europe's trade with the East.

Early History

In the fifth century the Huns invaded Aquileia, a flourishing city in northeastern Italy. The people of Aquileia fled and settled on nearby islands. The city of Venice probably formed on these islands in the mid-sixth century.

Early Venetian houses, built of wood, were erected on stilts above the water. As the first-settled islands grew more swampy and prone to malaria epidemics, the center of Venice moved from Torcello to its current position on the island of Rialto. Buildings had to be supported on piles driven several yards into the mud. Venetians moved around a system of canals by boat.

Growing Power

From 500 to 800, the Venetians, who had no land suitable for farming, made a living from fishing and producing salt. As they became richer, the Venetians were subject to attack. For protection Venice formed an alliance with the Byzantine Empire, based in Constantinople. In 810 Charlemagne, king of the Franks, concluded a treaty that recognized Venice's allegiance to Constantinople and upheld Venetian trading rights with the Italian mainland.

This image of St. Mark's Square in Venice, from a fifteenth-century French manuscript, includes St. Mark's Basilica (left), the Doge's Palace (right), and the campanile (bell tower; center foreground).

Between 800 and 1000, Venice built up its trading and shipping in the Adriatic Sea. In 1000 the Venetians defeated the Dalmatian pirates who harried their ships. Venice also took the Dalmatian coast, the eastern coast of the Adriatic, and thereby gained control of the sea routes to the Levant, the eastern Mediterranean coast. It was in the Levant that exotic goods arrived from all over Asia. Before long, Venetian ships were bringing these Asian goods to Venice. The city thus placed itself at the center of the trade between East and West.

Naval Supremacy

Venice rose to be the principal naval power in the Mediterranean. The navy defended Venetian shipping routes and profited from helping allies—notably the crusaders—in their wars. There was continual conflict between Venice and other cities in Italy,

THIS LETTER OF AROUND 523—FROM A ROMAN STATESMAN AND HISTORIAN WHOSE WRITINGS ARE A CRITICAL SOURCE OF INFORMATION FOR MODERN SCHOLARS—IS THE EARLIEST KNOWN DESCRIPTION OF VENICE:

Your ships fear not the harsh gusts . . . your houses [are] like aquatic birds, now on sea and now on shore. . . . The solid earth is there held together by woven willow boughs, and you have no doubts in opposing so frail a barrier to the waves, when the shore does not suffice, on account of its lowness, to hold back the mass of waters. Your inhabitants have abundance only of fish; rich and poor live together in equality . . . so they are free from the vice that rules the world.

CASSIODORUS, LETTER TO THE VENETIANS

A 1330 illustration of crusaders arriving at Constantinople in 1204. Venice played an instrumental role in the sacking of Constantinople.

CHRONOLOGY

421
According to traditional belief, Venice is founded.

697
The first doge is appointed.

810
Venice is recognized by Charlemagne as part of the Byzantine Empire.

1171
Power to appoint the doge is transferred from the people to the council.

1204
During the Fourth Crusade, Venice aids in the sacking of Constantinople.

1380
Venice defeats the Genoese navy at the Battle of Chioggia.

1497
Vasco da Gama's sea journey from Europe to India signals the end of Venetian dominance of trade.

VENICE 775

▲ *Saint Mark's Basilica was built in Venice in the eleventh century. Strong Byzantine influence in the decoration and architecture reflect Venice's links with Constantinople.*

enice was a republic; an elected head of state, the doge (duke), was assisted by a large council. Membership in the electorate and governing council was restricted to noble families. In 1172 electoral laws were introduced to keep doges from making the position hereditary. Most offices were held for a very short term, another measure intended to prevent corruption.

From 1310 an inner council, the Council of Ten, had considerably more power than the doge. The Ten, and the even more elite Council of Three, were widely feared for the their secret trials and summary executions.

particularly those that also depended on maritime trade. In 1380 Venice defeated Genoa, its great Italian rival for supremacy in the Mediterranean, at the Battle of Chioggia.

The Crusades
Venice made a fortune from providing crusaders with ships and establishing its own trading posts in the Levant. Booty pillaged from conquered lands added to Venice's wealth and adorned its increasingly ornate buildings.

In 1204 the soldiers of the Fourth Crusade, en route to Egypt, failed to pay money owed to Venice. It was agreed that the sacking of Constantinople, which had recently suffered a coup d'état, would serve in lieu of payment. After Constantinople fell, Venice took three-eighths of its lands, including the island of Crete.

Rise and Fall
The Venetian Republic was at its height in the fifteenth century. It maintained outposts all around the eastern Mediterranean, expanded into the Italian mainland, and took Cyprus in 1489. Bankers and merchants grew wealthy and built beautiful palaces. Venetian wealth was displayed in extravagant buildings and celebrations.

In 1497 the Portuguese sailor Vasco da Gama forged a direct sea route from Europe to Asia around the southern tip of Africa. During the sixteenth century European countries began to trade directly with East Asia. As the importance of the Levantine trading posts declined, so did Venice's power.

SEE ALSO
- Constantinople • Crusades
- Italian City-States • Ships and Seafaring
- Waterways

Vikings

THE VIKINGS FLOURISHED in Scandinavia from around 750 to 1100. Accomplished shipbuilders and navigators, ferocious warriors, and determined traders, Vikings raided in groups and often settled in the lands they attacked throughout Europe (the name Viking derives from the Norse word for "raid"). Vikings journeyed as far afield as North America, central Russia, and Constantinople. Originally pagans who worshiped numerous gods, they gradually converted to Christianity.

Viking Life

Although the word *Viking*, properly used, decribes only the raiding parties, it has been customary since the nineteenth century to refer to all early medieval Scandinavians as Vikings.

In their Scandinavian homelands (present-day Norway, Sweden, and Denmark), the Vikings lived by farming, hunting, and fishing. Viking society was organized into small communities. The Vikings made their own clothes, pots, and tools. Local chieftains each owned an area of land. All the chieftain's family members worked on the farm, where they grew oats and barley and raised cattle, pigs, chickens, and geese. A rich chieftain would keep slaves to carry out the more arduous jobs on the farms and to serve in his house.

Viking families lived in longhouses, dwellings that measured between fifty and one hundred feet (15–30 m) in length and were usually built from wood and thatched with straw. A longhouse had a large central hall in which everyone ate, slept, and worked. In winter the animals were brought indoors and kept in an enclosure at one end of the house.

Viking chiefs held their feasts in massive wooden halls. This reconstructed feasting hall was built on the site of a Viking fort in Fyrkat, Denmark.

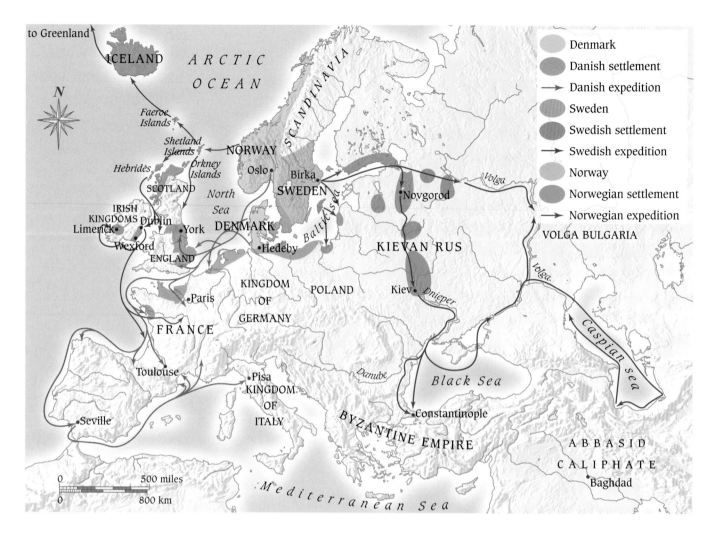

to Greenland

ICELAND

ARCTIC

OCEAN

N

Faeroe Islands

Shetland Islands

Hebrides

Orkney Islands

SCOTLAND

North Sea

IRISH KINGDOMS Dublin

Limerick

Wexford

ENGLAND

York

NORWAY

Oslo

Birka

SWEDEN

Baltic Sea

Novgorod

Volga

KIEVAN RUS

VOLGA BULGARIA

DENMARK

Hedeby

Kiev

Dnieper

Paris

KINGDOM OF GERMANY

POLAND

Volga

Caspian Sea

FRANCE

Toulouse

Pisa

KINGDOM OF ITALY

Danube

Black Sea

BYZANTINE EMPIRE

Constantinople

Seville

ABBASID CALIPHATE

Baghdad

Mediterranean Sea

	Denmark
	Danish settlement
→	Danish expedition
	Sweden
	Swedish settlement
→	Swedish expedition
	Norway
	Norwegian settlement
→	Norwegian expedition

0 500 miles
0 800 km

▲ *The Vikings traveled great distances from their Scandinavian homeland on missions whose primary purpose was sometimes trade, sometimes pillage.*

Viking families held great feasts in the longhouses to celebrate religious festivals and military victories. A funeral was also an occasion for a lavish feast. Acrobats and jugglers performed at feasts, which often lasted for days, and skalds (poet-singers) recited part-historical, part-mythical poems and tales about the adventures of great Viking heroes.

Boats and Ships

Vikings constructed sturdy merchant ships, known as knarrs, which were used by traders and settlers. A wide vessel with a deep hull, a knarr could carry thirty or forty people as well as animals and food supplies. It was equipped with both oars and sails and could undertake long and dangerous sea journeys.

The most famous Viking ships are the longships, the ships of war. These long, slender vessels could travel very swiftly but were also light enough to be carried across ground. Designed to sail up shallow rivers or land on sloping beaches, longships enabled the Vikings to launch surprise attacks. Sometimes known as dragon ships on account of a tall prow that was carved in the shape of a fierce dragon or bird, longships had up to seventy oars as well as a large sail. The mast could easily be taken down. A longship was steered by a single steering oar attached to the right side (the steer board, or starboard) of the ship.

Viking Raiders

Between 793 and 900, Vikings launched numerous raids on the coasts of Britain and

France. Although at first they sought only plunder and slaves, it seems that when they found the opposition weak, some Vikings decided to seize enemy land. Some raiders reached Spain and even Italy. They usually landed secretly by night and then fought their way inland, robbing towns and villages as they went.

Vikings warriors were feared all over Europe. Trained since boyhood to follow their chieftain into battle, they usually fought with axes, javelins, and swords. Most Viking warriors wore leather tunics and round metal helmets. Certain ferocious soldiers, called berserkers, wore bearskins. The soldiers' name, which derives from Old Norse words that mean "bear shirt," survives in the English word *berserk*, denoting a state of frenzied violence. Certain berserkers may even have fought naked.

Many Viking raiders settled in the countries they attacked. In general, Viking communitites outside of Scandinavia were based around farming. Notable Viking settlements grew up in northern France (where the Vikings became known as Normans), eastern England, southern Ireland, and northern Scotland.

Settlers and Explorers

Boatloads of traders and settlers made their way along the rivers of Russia. As they moved south, they conquered Finnish and Slavic settlements and seized furs and slaves. Some Vikings continued beyond Russia, at times carrying their boats overland until they reached the next river. Eventually these Vikings found their way to the Black Sea.

Other Viking explorers sailed west across the Atlantic Ocean. After a Viking colony was established on Iceland, some explorers traveled even farther west. In 985

VIKING RELIGION

The Vikings believed that their gods and goddesses controlled all aspects of life. The Viking, or Norse, gods lived in a heavenly place called Asgard but often visited the world of humans, known as Midgard. Some gods controlled the crops and weather, while others were gods of war. The chief god, Odin, ruled over Valhalla, a hall where heroic warriors slain in battle spent eternity feasting and hunting and fighting. Other Viking gods included Thor, the god of thunder, and Freya, the goddess of fertility.

◀ *This eighth-century carved memorial stone, found in Gotland, Sweden, marked the burial place of a Viking chief. Depicted on it are legends of the gods, Viking invaders in longships, and a battle scene.*

the Norwegian leader Erik the Red established a colony in Greenland. Erik's son, Leif Eriksson, reached the coast of North America around 1000. The land he found, which he named Vinland (land of grapes), was probably present-day Newfoundland.

▲ *A photograph of a twelfth-century stave church at Gol, in Norway. The distinctive structure of stave churches was probably influenced by the wooden temples that the Vikings built for their gods.*

SKALDS AND SAGAS

Viking poets, known as skalds, recited sagas, long narrative poems that told the stories of Norse gods and heroes. The sagas were first written down in Iceland around 1150. One of the most famous is the *Heimskringla* of Snorri Sturluson, which celebrates the battles and achievements of the Norwegian kings. Two Icelandic sagas, the *Saga of Erik the Red* and the *Saga of the Greenlanders*, describe the journeys of two great Viking explorers Erik the Red (who colonized Greenland) and his son Lief Eriksson, who sailed to North America.

A group of settlers tried to establish a colony there, but they were driven away by the local Native Americans.

Viking Merchants

Viking merchants sold furs and wine as well as carved objects, weapons, and jewelry made by craft workers. Slave trading was an extremely important part of Viking life. Some traders were based in Viking towns, such as Hedeby (in Denmark), Birka (in Sweden), York (in England), and Novgorod (in Russia). Others traveled from place to place. Viking merchants traded throughout western Europe. Some of them made the long journey through Russia to the great Byzantine capital of Constantinople (present-day Istanbul, in Turkey), while a few even reached the Abbasid capital, Baghdad (in present-day Iraq).

Christianization and Assimilation

The Viking gods were generally warlike and fierce—a reflection, perhaps, of the Viking way of life. However, as the Vikings made contact with other lands, they gradually adopted Christian beliefs. Around 965, Harald Bluetooth, king of Denmark, converted to Christianity; over the next fifty years, the other Viking kingdoms also became Christian. As Vikings were assimilated into local populations, their way of life became more settled and peaceful. By around 1100 the Viking raids that for so long disrupted life in Europe had come to an end.

SEE ALSO

- Denmark • Exploration • Iceland
- Norway • Novgorod • Ships and Seafaring
- Sweden

Visigothic Spain

THE IBERIAN PENINSULA, comprising the modern-day countries of Spain and Portugal, was dominated by the Visigoths, a tribe of Germanic origin, during the sixth and seventh centuries. The rule of the Visigoths lasted until the early eighth century, when they were defeated at the hands of Muslims invading from North Africa.

Sometime during the early fourth century the Goths, an eastern Germanic people, divided into two branches—the Ostrogoths and Visigoths. The two peoples shared family connections and remained on friendly terms.

During the fourth century the power of the Roman Empire began to decline. In 410 the Visigoths invaded Italy and sacked the city of Rome itself. In order to regain control of their imperial heartland, the Romans offered the Visigoths territory in Gaul (present-day France) and Spain. In order to claim their Spanish territory, the Visigoths first had to drive out the Vandals.

By 429 the Visigoths had succeeded in forcing the Vandals out of Spain, and by the late fifth century they controlled a large area of southwestern Gaul and most of the Iberian Peninsula. Only the kingdom of the Sueves in northeastern Spain held out. The Visigothic king Euric (reigned 466–c. 484) established his capital at Toulouse, in southern Gaul.

Attacks from North and South

The Visigoths' territory in Gaul soon came under attack from the Franks. In 507 Alaric II lost nearly all his lands north of the Pyrenees Mountains to the new arrivals. The Ostrogoths helped to protect the Visigoths from further Frankish incursions, and a new Visigothic capital was established at Toledo, in central Spain.

In 552 armies of the Byzantine (Eastern Roman) Empire conquered Visigothic lands

This Visigothic church, the oldest church on the Iberian Peninsula, was built in 661 in Baños de Cerrato, near the modern city of Palencia.

▶ *This cross, studded with stones, is from the mid-seventh century, a time when the Visigoths had firm control of the entire Iberian Peninsula.*

theless bore some Roman influence. The Visigoths did not attempt to impose their laws on their Spanish subjects, who had for so long been governed according to the laws of the Roman Empire. In 506 King Alaric II issued the Lex Romana Visigothorum, an essentially Roman code by which Hispano-Romans were to be governed.

In 654 King Recceswinth issued the Liber Judiciorum, a law code whose terms bound all people living in Visigothic territory. The new code built on previous changes to the law—including the sanction of intermarriage between Visigoths and Romans—and tended to improve the sense of unity between the Visigothic rulers and their formerly Roman subjects.

The Visigoths and Arianism

Originally, the Visigoths followed Arianism, a version of Christianity that was condemned as heretical in 325. One of the Arians' key beliefs was that Jesus was, not a truly divine being who shared in the essence of God, but a created being and thus inferior to God. After they moved to Spain, many Visigoths began to convert to orthodox Catholicism. Although some Arian rulers persecuted Catholics, they failed to stop the movement away from Arianism.

The last king to make a stand for Arianism was Leovigild, who ruled from 568 to 586. Although he tried to stop his subjects from repudiating Arianism, many Visigoths had already converted. The converts included one of Leovigild's own sons, who led a rebellion against him. Though Leovigild defeated the uprising, his victory was short-lived. His heir, Recared, embraced Catholicism when he ascended the throne in 587. In a major church

in southern Spain. In 585 the Visigoths conquered the Sueves, and by 625 they had succeeded in expelling the Byzantines from the south.

Visigothic Law

In the fifth century Euric had drawn up a law code, called the Codex Euricianum. Essentially Germanic, Euric's code never-

VISIGOTHIC SOCIETY

The society of the Visigoths was hierarchical (that is, it was rigidly structured according to rank). At the top of the hierarchy was the king; next were the high and low nobles, followed by freemen and finally slaves. There were further hierarchies within this broad system. For example, a king's slave had higher rank than any other slave.

A person was not necessarily confined permanently to his or her particular place in the hierarchy. It was possible to move from one level to another—especially downward. Freemen and even nobles could be enslaved as a punishment for crime or an unpaid debt or after being captured in war. Although rare, it was theoretically possible to move upward. The child of a slave could become free, for example. Thus, there was scope within the Visigothic social system for an individual to improve greatly his or her circumstances.

council held at Toledo in 589, Catholicism was declared the kingdom's official religion. Arianism soon disappeared entirely.

The End of Visigothic Spain

The common law code and shared religion helped unify the Visigothic and Roman people. Nevertheless, a series of internal problems, brought about by the Visigothic system of government, soon broke the power of the kingdom.

The powerful Visigothic nobles had never accepted a hereditary monarchy, in which power passed from a king to his descendants. Instead, they favored the old Germanic system, in which the nobles selected one of their own number to be king. The old system had serious disadvantages, however: conflict almost inevitably arose when a king died, as the powerful nobles vied with each other to become the new king. Because the Visigoths spent much time mired in internal conflicts, they became vulnerable to outside threats.

◀ This seventh-century bronze belt buckle includes animal designs in each of its four sections.

By the end of the seventh century, Visigothic Spain was riven by internal rebellions and civil war. In 711 Muslims from North Africa landed in Spain. One of the Visigothic factions competing for power asked the Muslims for support. The new invaders soon began to take power into their own hands. The divided Visigoths could not mount an effective defense (some of them even seem to have sided with the Muslims) and were quickly conquered.

▲ *The cross-shaped church of San Pedro de la Nave is located in a town near present-day Zamora, Spain.*

MIXED TRADITIONS

Visigothic traditions were a combination of Germanic and Roman practices. Visigothic kings maintained the old Germanic belief that a king should be a strong military leader. From the Romans the Visigoths adopted the view that a ruler was responsible for the health and well-being of his subjects and the good order of his society. The Roman system of administration also provided a model for many of the structures that the Visigoths used to govern their lands.

The Visigoths found a haven in a small unconquered region in the northwest of Spain that became the Kingdom of Asturias. The Muslims also allowed Visigothic subjects to continue their traditional practices in Muslim-ruled lands. Visigothic influence endured in Spain long after the defeat by the Muslims. One of the principles that guided the *Reconquista* (the long Christian campaign to expel the Muslims from Spain) was the desire to make Spain once more a Christian territory—as it had been under the Visigoths.

SEE ALSO
- Goths • Islam • Legal Codes
- Reconquista • Spanish Kingdoms
- Umayyads • Vandals

CHRONOLOGY

507
Expelled from Gaul by the Franks, the Visigoths secure most of the Iberian Peninsula.

552
Byzantines conquer southern Spain.

585
Visigoths conquer the Sueves.

589
Reject Arianism and adopt Catholicism.

625
Regain control of southern Spain.

654
Establish a legal code that binds all people in their territory.

711
Muslims invade and quickly conquer Spain.

Wales

IN THE FIFTH CENTURY CE, Britain was invaded by Germanic tribes who became known collectively as Anglo-Saxons. The native Britons were forced to the western and southwestern extremes of the island; those in the west began to form a new nation. While the Anglo-Saxons called them Welsh ("foreigners"), the Britons called themselves Cymry ("fellow countrymen"). Medieval Wales, never a single united state, was a collection of small kingdoms or principalities that expanded and contracted over time.

Norman Invasions

After their conquest of England in 1066, the Normans created three earldoms on the Welsh borders. These earldoms were used as bases for repeated invasions of Wales. Between 1067 and 1154, periods of swift Norman advance alternated with major retreats. The Normans were able to hold only the Welsh lowlands and river valleys.

Expansion of Gwynedd

In the thirteenth century two rulers of the northern Welsh principality of Gwynedd, Llywelyn the Great (reigned 1196–1240) and his grandson Llywelyn ap Gruffudd (1246–1282), created a state strong enough to resist further Anglo-Norman incursions.

Llywelyn ap Gruffudd's mistake was to make an enemy of King Edward I of England (reigned 1272–1307). Llywelyn refused to pay Edward homage, an official ceremony in which he would have recognized Edward as his overlord. In two swift campaigns, in 1276 and in 1282 and 1283, Edward conquered the whole of Wales. Llywelyn was killed in battle, and his head was displayed on a pole in London.

▶ *Llywelyn the Great's son, Gruffudd, spent three years as a prisoner of Henry III. In 1244 he fell to his death while trying to flee the Tower of London, a scene depicted in this contemporary illumination.*

Harlech Castle, built in the 1280s, was part of a powerful chain of fortifications planned by King Edward I to pin down the Welsh in the north. In the early 1400s Harlech was the headquarters of the Welsh leader Owain Glyndwr.

Edward spent vast sums of money building a chain of ten great castles to control the Welsh. The lands around the castles and the new towns founded by Edward were cleared of the native population, who were replaced by English settlers.

Owain Glyndwr

In 1400 Welsh resentment at English rule sparked a great rebellion, led by Owain Glyndwr, a descendant of the royal family of Powys. By 1404 Owain controlled most of the country as prince of Wales. He began forming alliances with England's enemies, Scotland and France. The following year, Prince Henry (later King Henry V) invaded Wales and defeated Owain in battle. Owain fled north, from where he continued to fight a guerilla war until 1410, when he disappeared from history. There were no further major uprisings against English rule.

SEE ALSO
- Anglo-Saxons
- England

CHRONOLOGY

1067
Normans invade Wales.

1196–1240
Under Llywelyn the Great, Gwynedd is strengthened.

1246–1282
Llywelyn ap Gruffudd rules most of northern and western Wales.

1283
Edward I of England completes his conquest of Wales.

1301
Edward I makes his son, the future king Edward II, prince of Wales.

1400–1410
Owain Glyndwr fights a war of independence.

Warfare

IN MEDIEVAL SOCIETIES WORLDWIDE, disputes over land ownership or control of natural resources might lead to hostilities ranging from skirmishes between neighbors to pitched battles between rival rulers. Warfare (whatever its underlying cause) plays havoc with lives and social arrangements. After the year 1000, in a Europe disfigured by centuries of strife and invasion, warfare for a time became limited and regulated, and opponents, thanks partly to religious pressure, began to fight according to agreed-upon rules.

Setting Limits to War

During the early Middle Ages in Europe, warfare and instability sometimes seemed inescapable. As early as the fourth century Saint Augustine and other Christian writers began framing rules to limit war's scope and devastation. They wrote that to be just, a war could be proclaimed only by someone in authority; that it must have a good cause, a good goal, and a real chance of success; and that combatants must act with restraint.

In Christian Europe the church tried to limit warfare further by inducing local rulers to swear to keep the Truce of God, whose terms prohibited fighting on Sundays, Fridays, and days of special religious observance. The church sought especially to shield noncombatants—women, children, the elderly, and priests, monks, and nuns.

Other rules and humane conventions came into being. From the outset of a siege, heralds, protected by a safe-conduct, could move between the fortress and the attack-

◀ *This illustration of a seventh-century Muslim siege of Constantinople, the capital of the Byzantine Empire, is part of a thirteenth-century Spanish manuscript, the* Cantigas de Santa María.

ing army in order to discuss surrender terms. Once terms had been agreed upon, they were kept. Only if the fortress was taken by storm were the attackers allowed to plunder it and kill the defenders. There were also codes governing the treatment of prisoners of war, as well as their exchange or ransom, and the safety of hostages.

Battles, too, had rules and conventions. Cavalry charges were violent and were meant to be deadly, but once opposing warriors were fighting one-on-one, each became much more concerned to capture than kill his enemy, since a captured enemy could be held for ransom. This conduct, originating in mercenary motives, became part of the knightly code of chivalry as a principle of mercy.

Recruitment and Organization

In feudal Europe the leaders of an army were the nobility, who owed military service to their lord in return for the land he had granted them. A noble could in turn order his tenants to fight for him, and so the chain of command continued down to the level of the peasant farmers.

The system of military recruitment was bound by strict rules. A given fief, or land-holding, was reckoned to be worth a certain number of fully equipped knights, and a lord could not demand any more than that number of a vassal. Similarly, peasants could not be forced to serve any longer than a fixed time period.

Since it was in nobody's interest to keep an army in the field at harvest time, armies would disband for the winter. Thus, the campaigning season was only a few months long. In the later Middle Ages rulers began to employ mercenaries, men who fought for pay and might be recruited from abroad. The Swiss in particular had a reputation as fearless soldiers and efficient mercenaries.

Campaigning

After soldiers were recruited, they had to be equipped. The cavalry (mounted knights) required horses, armor, lances, swords, and shields; the infantry (peasant foot soldiers) were supplied with bows and arrows and such other weapons as pikes and axes. The men needed food to sustain themselves, and the horses needed fodder.

▶ *An English soldier is killed by a Norman invader at the Battle of Hastings. The Normans' conquest of England (1066) was recorded on the Bayeux tapestry, of which this scene forms a part.*

A thirteenth-century manuscript illustration of Spanish Moors, having regained lost territory, returning home with their animals.

All supplies had to be transported, and so an army on the march would be accompanied by pack animals and wagons, as well as servants and squires. Scouts and outriders watched for enemy ambushes, and spies were sent into enemy territory to look for vulnerable areas.

The commander had to decide on long-term campaign strategy and tactics for any military emergency. Generally commanders tried to avoid pitched battles and to concentrate their strength on sieges instead. A successful siege might result in the capture of a building of great strategic or political importance (a castle, for example) and, if swiftly concluded, was much less damaging to the besieging army.

Sometimes, however, battle could not be avoided. To win a battle, it was important to try to gain any advantage from the terrain. For example, the cavalry might take up position at the top of a slope in order to charge downhill, or archers might conceal themselves in a wood and wait for the enemy cavalry to draw level before bringing them down with their arrows.

A SYRIAN BISHOP AND HISTORIAN WROTE THE FOLLOWING ACCOUNT OF THE CAPTURE OF HIS HOME TOWN OF TYRE BY CRUSADERS IN 1124:

Both sides agreed that the city should be handed over to the Christians, with free egress granted to the citizens, their wives and children and all their wealth. . . . But when the people of the lower sort realized . . . they took it badly that the city should be surrendered on these terms, and that it would not be available for them to smash up violently for plunder. . . . Nevertheless, the saner mentality of their superiors prevailed, and when the city was surrendered, freedom to leave was given to the citizens, as agreed.

WILLIAM OF TYRE

▲ *This illustration, from a 1483 manuscript called the* Berner Chronik, *depicts the Battle of Granson (1476), in which a force of Swiss footsoldiers scored a spectacular victory over the more formidable looking Burgundian army.*

WARFARE IN POLYNESIA

Throughout the scattered islands of Poynesia, a vast triangle of the Pacific Ocean settled between around 1000 BCE and 1000 CE, intertribal warfare was extremely common, particularly in areas where populations had grown large and resources were limited. Polynesians fought with heavy wooden clubs, spears, and throwing stones. Before a battle, the temple of the god of war would be refurbished or even rebuilt. Warfare was accompanied by elaborate religious rituals, and captured opponents would often be sacrificed to the gods. In some cases, a victorious warrior would eat a powerful defeated opponent in the belief that he would thus absorb his victim's mana (spiritual power).

A navy could be immensely useful if a commander fighting far from home needed provisions. Supply fleets would often find themselves under attack by enemy ships or by pirates. Although the Mongols were extremely successful warriors on horseback, their failure to develop a navy is often cited as a major reason why they were eventually defeated by the Mamluks.

The End of the Middle Ages

By the fifteenth century the nature of European warfare had changed. The feudal pattern of land tenure had broken down; a lord could no longer call on the service of his tenant, nor could the tenant on the peasant. Instead, great nobles and emerging nations maintained full-time armies or employed mercenaries.

Weapons and armor in Europe had also changed with the introduction of gunpowder from China and the subsequent use of primitive guns and cannons. When the first Europeans arrived in the Americas in the last years of the fifteenth century, they encountered native peoples who waged war without guns and horses. The new arrivals' use of these technologically advanced methods of warfare gave them an overwhelming advantage.

SEE ALSO
- Arms and Armor • Battles • Cavalry
- Chivalry • Knights • Mamluks
- Mongols • Samurai • Shoguns
- Sieges

Waterways

GOODS WERE OFTEN CARRIED by water in the Middle Ages, whether across the sea, along naturally occurring rivers and lakes, or through artificial canals. Trading routes and major towns usually grew up along the course of rivers. The most advanced engineering techniques for building canals, dams, locks, dikes, and irrigation systems were found in China.

Canals and Rivers in China

The Chinese were using an advanced system of canals before the Middle Ages. The Grand Canal, which runs from Beijing to Hangzhou, includes the oldest sections of canal in the world. Although most of the Grand Canal was built in 605 CE, parts of it were constructed as early as 486 BCE.

The most important rivers in China are the Huang He (Yellow River) and Chang Jiang, or Yangtze, both of which run from west to east across the country. The Huang He changed its course dramatically in 1194, when it took over the Huai River drainage system—a situation that lasted for the next seven hundred years. Rivers and canals were the only practical way for people and goods to cross the vast country.

The Vikings in Russia

Great seafarers, the Vikings traveled around the Baltic and Mediterranean seas in Europe and across the Atlantic Ocean to Iceland, Greenland, and even North America. From the mid-eighth century to the late eleventh, they traded along the rivers of northern Europe and traveled through Russia and as far as Constantinople

◀ A painting on silk of the boat of the Sui dynasty emperor Yangdi (560–618 CE) on the Chinese Grand Canal.

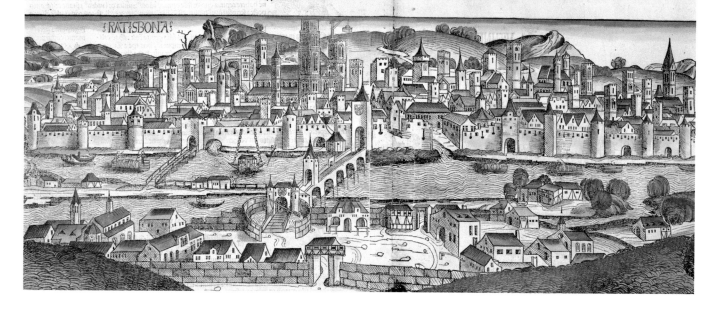

RATISBONA

▲ *A prime position on the Danube River made the ancient settlement of Ratisbon, in southeastern Germany, an extremely prosperous city in the twelfth and thirteenth centuries. Its stone bridge (pictured at the center of this woodcut from the fifteenth-century Nuremberg Chronicle), built between 1135 and 1146, was renowned throughout Europe.*

and Baghdad. Goods to be sold were carried from Scandinavia in Viking seagoing ships for the first part of the journey and then moved into flat-bottomed boats that could navigate the shallower and narrower channels inland. The Vikings traveled along Russian rivers to the Black and Caspian seas, where they joined trade routes to China and the East.

European Waterways

Many of Europe's principal rivers were used for transport before Roman times. In western Europe the Rhine and the Danube were particularly important trade and transport routes. Many goods were carried around the coast of Great Britain by ship, and ships also traveled along the Atlantic coasts of France and Spain.

In low-lying areas whose land was close to sea level, canal systems were built during the Middle Ages. Europe's most famous canal system is in Venice, a city built on a group of islands. In northern Europe people living in the low-lying areas of the Netherlands, Flanders, and East Anglia (in eastern England) also created systems of canals and dikes (drainage ditches). In these areas, which were prone to flooding,

AZTEC WATERWAYS

The Aztec capital, Tenochtitlán, was built in 1325 on islands in Lake Texcoco, in central Mexico. Since the city was crisscrossed by canals and bridges, European visitors likened it to Venice. Everything traveling to and from the city was either ferried across the lake or brought into the city across a causeway that linked Tenochtitlán to the shore.

The Valley of Mexico had several naturally occurring waterways. The Aztecs extended these waterways to create an advanced system of canals, along which food could be brought from agricultural land elsewhere in the empire to the capital.

local people traveled in flat-bottomed boats and often navigated across flooded fields and fens (marshes), as well as along the canals, rivers, and dikes.

SEE ALSO

William the Conqueror

WILLIAM THE CONQUEROR (c. 1027–1087) became duke of Normandy (in northern France) in 1035. In 1066 he defeated the Anglo-Saxons at the Battle of Hastings. As King William I of England, he helped establish the feudal pattern of land tenure. He left a legacy of strong royal government and made Norman French the language of English aristocratic society.

Duke of Normandy

Born around 1028, the illegitimate son of Duke Robert I of Normandy, William was sometimes known to his contemporaries as William the Bastard. Nevertheless, following his father's death in 1035, William was recognized as heir to the duchy. At first, William's great-uncle ruled on his behalf, but by the age of nineteen, the young duke was fully in charge. He dealt successfully with rebellions and with threats from neighboring nobles, including an attack from the king of France.

William's Plans

By the 1060s Duke William was known as an efficient but ruthless ruler. He had built up a skilled army and was married to the wealthy Matilda of Flanders. However, he still planned to expand his dominions.

William claimed that his distant cousin, Edward the Confessor of England, had promised that William would succeed to the English throne after Edward's death. In 1064 William tricked Earl Harold of Wessex into swearing allegiance to him. Therefore, when Harold succeeded Edward

William the Conqueror gave orders for strong castles to be built in strategic positions throughout his newly conquered kingdom. Rochester Castle in Kent, pictured here, was begun in 1087 by William's architect, Bishop Gundulf.

WILLIAM WAS GENERALLY CONSIDERED A TOUGH, EVEN RUTHLESS RULER:

Assuredly in his time, men suffered grievous oppression and manifold injuries. He caused castles to be built which were a sore burden to the poor.

ANGLO-SAXON CHRONICLE

▲ *The key events of William's conquest of England are depicted in the Bayeux tapestry, which was begun around 1067. In this scene Norman troops are depicted crossing the English Channel.*

as king of England in January 1066, William decided to invade England and stake his claim to the throne.

The Conquest

After seven months of preparation, the Normans sailed for England in around six hundred transport ships, which carried more than seven thousand men and two thousand horses.

William landed unopposed on the coast of southern England and set up camp at Hastings. King Harold and his army had just defeated an attempted invasion by the king of Norway at the Battle of Stamford Bridge, near York, hundreds of miles to the north. Harold's men were forced to march south as fast as they could. By the time they arrived in Hastings on October 14, 1066, they were exhausted. They fought fiercely, but by the end of the day, King Harold had been killed,

and William's forces had won the Battle of Hastings.

Establishing Control

William was crowned king of England on Christmas Day in 1066, but it was six years before he would secure his position in the face of near-continual attacks, especially along the Welsh marches (borderlands). To help safeguard his kingdom, William granted land to Norman barons, who built strong castles along the threatened frontiers.

Throughout England, William confiscated land from the Anglo-Saxon earls and gave it to his Norman barons, who promised to fight for him in return. Although a system of service in return for land was already operating in England, William's arrangement marked the true beginning of English feudalism.

In order to establish a system of taxation in his new domain, William set up a survey of all the land in England. The resulting document became known as the Domesday Book. William maintained strong law and order. He kept many of the Anglo-Saxon laws and gained control of the church by installing French-speaking bishops.

SEE ALSO

- **Anglo-Saxons** • **Battles** • **Bayeux Tapestry**
- **Domesday Book** • **Normans**

Women

IN MEDIEVAL EUROPE, queens and noblewomen played a key role in politics, and ladies of the manor ran the household. In the countryside women labored on the land and tended animals, while in towns they were often employed as craft workers and shopkeepers. In most parts of the world, girls received less education than boys; nevertheless, some women made outstanding achievements in academic and artistic fields. Women enjoyed a particularly high status at the Japanese court and in the African kingdom of Benin.

Women in the Family

Generally speaking, in medieval Europe a woman's status in society depended on that of her husband. Most women married, and a husband's duty was to support his wife materially. The usual prospect for a rich unmarried woman was life as a nun, while poorer unmarried women frequently worked as servants.

It was customary for a daughter's marriage to be arranged by her family. It was not unusual among wealthy families for a teenage girl to marry an older man. A young wife usually began having children in her teens and was expected to bear many children (half or more of her children were likely to die before adulthood). While women often died in labor, mortality rates were also very high for men, and many women were widowed young. Divorce was prohibited by the church, although a man with influence could sometimes have a marriage annulled, especially if his wife had borne him no children.

Poor Women

In less wealthy families a wife ran the home and helped her husband with his work. A wife living in the country would be responsible for cultivating a vegetable garden and keeping chickens or geese, a cow, and perhaps some pigs. She prepared and

▲ *A fifteenth-century miniature of women picking sage leaves. Many women in Europe tended their own garden and worked in the fields.*

In medieval towns, women often worked in the family shop or workshop. There are numerous records of wives and daughters working as bakers, brewers, and potters. Some women worked as goldsmiths, painters, and in other skilled crafts. Some found work as midwives or weavers. A large number of women, in both town and country, were employed as servants for prosperous or wealthy families.

Rich Women

The wife of a wealthy man ran her husband's household and supervised the servants. The lady of the manor instructed her cook as to which dishes to prepare, controlled the household budget, and made sure that guests were well looked after. Men spent long periods of time away at war; in their absence a wife took responsibility for the running of the estate lands and the welfare of the tenants.

In addition to household duties, a wealthy woman was also responsible for supervising the education of her children—her daughters in particular. Among the pastimes with which a noblewoman filled her leisure time were music, singing, embroidery, chess and other games, and even falconry.

Wealthy noblewomen often took a keen interest in politics. The wife of a man with political responsibility might be consulted by her husband and thus play a vital role behind the scenes. Mothers also influenced sons, even after they had grown up.

One particularly influential medieval woman was Eleanor of Aquitaine. Eleanor, a wealthy landowner in her own right, was married first to King Louis VII of France and then to King Henry II of England. Eleanor played a key role in French and English politics and even supported two of

In this 1475 French miniature, a maidservant shares secrets with her mistress.

cooked meals, made the family's clothes, and cared for her children. At busy times in the farming year, she helped out in the fields. Many women also had the task of selling produce at market.

CHRISTINE DE PISAN 1364–c. 1430

Christine de Pisan was the daughter of an Italian physician who worked at the French court. She married a French nobleman but, at the age of twenty-five, was widowed and left with three children to support.

Christine found many patrons for her writing at the court of King Charles VI. She produced several volumes of poetry, including *La cité des dames (The City of Ladies)*, a dream vision of a perfect city inhabited by powerful, educated women. In 1418 Christine retired to a convent, where she continued to write. One of her last works was a tribute to Joan of Arc, the heroine who led a French force to victory against the English during the Hundred Years War. Christine saw Joan as a model of female courage.

her sons, Richard and John, in a rebellion against their father, Henry.

Women and Education

In medieval Europe most girls from poor farming families grew up unable to read or write. A girl learning a trade or craft might acquire basic arithmetic and reading skills on the job. A wealthy girl, however, had more opportunities. The daughter of a king or a noble would be educated at home by a tutor—usually a member of the clergy.

Although girls could not attend university, some were able to pursue studies during a period of withdrawal from society for religious reasons. Hildegard of Bingen, (1098–1179), for example, a famously learned nun, wrote books on religion, compiled an encyclopedia of the natural world, and composed church music. Juliana of Norwich (c. 1342–c. 1416), who was an anchorite—a kind of hermit—wrote a powerful visionary poem, *The Revelation of Divine Love*. The influential French poet Christine de Pisan spent her later life in a convent.

▶ *In this fourteenth-century German manuscript illustration, a noblewoman is depicted playing chess with the Holy Roman emperor Otto IV.*

Sacred and Secular Perspectives

The Bible has no single "view" of women. In Genesis, Eve is the fatal temptress of Adam, by whom sin came into the world, whereas in the New Testament, the Virgin Mary is the conduit to human redemption from sin. In everyday practice the church saw men and women as having characteristic vices (and virtues). For example, women were thought more prone to vanity, deceit, and seduction and are so described in religious poems and writings.

Secular medieval literature has its own varied slants. Such popular romances as the *Roman de la rose* and *Le Morte d'Arthur* promote the ideal of courtly love, wherein a chivalrous knight's devotion to a perfect and often unattainable lady borders on reverence. Idealized portraits of women also appear in medieval literature, paintings, and songs.

▼ *This twelfth-century Chinese painting shows ladies of the court preparing silk, a common pastime among noblewomen.*

Women in Japan

In medieval Japan women at the imperial court were highly educated. They composed poetry and music and met to discuss their work. One such courtly lady, Murasaki Shikibu (c. 978–1015), is gener-

AFRICAN QUEEN MOTHERS

In the West African kingdom of Benin, queen mothers, known as *iyobas,* had enormous power. After the *iyoba* bore the ruler his first son, she had no other children. Thenceforth, she devoted her life to raising the future ruler of the kingdom. During her lifetime the *iyoba* was treated as a semidivine being, one who could protect the future ruler from evil. After her death she was worshiped as a goddess.

ally considered the world's first novelist. In *The Tale of Genji*, Murasaki includes vivid descriptions of life among the wealthy in medieval Japan that have been invaluable to scholars and historians.

Glossary

burgher An inhabitant of a town or borough; typically, a prosperous and respectable citizen.

canonize To officially declare that a deceased man or woman is a Christian saint (the term refers to the entering of the person's name in the canon, or list, of the saints).

census An official count of the population (often done during the Middle Ages to register people on tax rolls).

challenge In a tournament, a formal invitation to engage in combat.

corvée A form of labor, usually road building or other construction work, that is levied as or in lieu of a tax payment. The corvée was part of the obligation of a vassal to a feudal lord.

crank A kind of simple machine: a device that converts circular movement into back-and-forth movement, or vice versa.

dhow A light yet strong wooden sailing ship with a lateen (triangular) sail that was used by medieval Arab traders.

dike An embankment built to prevent flooding; also, an artificial watercourse (a ditch).

divan In the Ottoman Empire, the sultan's court or privy council.

exchequer Originally, the checked cloth on which an English king's accounts were settled; later, the government department responsible for managing royal revenues.

geomancy A form of divination that uses geographical features and phenomena to predict the future or uncover hidden knowledge.

junk A wooden sailing ship with a high stern and slatted sails that was used in medieval China (and even down to the present).

litter A curtained couch, carried by porters in the manner of a stretcher, on which a monarch or high-ranking official was transported in medieval China and the Incan Empire of Peru.

loom A frame on which threads are woven into cloth.

numerology A branch of learning that assumes that numbers have mystical or divine significance and studies them to understand it.

pagan A person adhering to a polytheistic religion (that is, one involving many gods).

pagoda A tall, slender, multistoried tower, with roofs that project and curve upward at each level, commonly built as a temple in East Asia.

pas d'armes A kind of tournament especially common in medieval Burgundy, in which a knight holds a piece of ground against all comers.

poleax A staff weapon with, usually, an ax blade backed by a hammer and topped by a spike or else with a hammer backed by a beak.

portico A colonnaded, roofed structure, often at the entrance to a building.

Scholasticism The leading school of medieval European philosophy; Scholastics (or Schoolmen) studied and interpreted Christian dogma in the light of earlier Christian and ancient Greek thought, especially that of Aristotle.

squire A young man who is attendant upon a knight and may himself be a knight in training.

stupa A domed Buddhist shrine.

tally A piece of notched wood used to record a financial transaction.

tithe Literally, "tenth"; a portion of money or goods paid as a tax, usually to the church.

vizier In the Ottoman Empire, a chief minister or high civil official.

Index

Page numbers in **boldface** type refer to main articles.
Page numbers in *italic* type refer to illustrations.